Raising and Praising Boys

Elizabeth Hartley Brewer

Vermilion
LONDON

3 5 7 9 10 8 6 4 2

First published in the United Kingdom in 2005 by Vermilion,
an imprint of Ebury Publishing
Random House UK Ltd
Random House, 20 Vauxhall Bridge Road, London SW1V 2SA

Random House Australia (Pty) Limited
20 Alfred Street, Milsons Point, Sydney, New South Wales 2061, Australia

Random House New Zealand Limited
18 Poland Road, Glenfield, Auckland 10, New Zealand

Random House (Pty) Limited
Isle of Houghton, Corner of Boundary Road & Carse O'Gowrie,
Houghton 2198, South Africa

Random House UK Limited Reg. No. 954009
www.randomhouse.co.uk
Papers used by Vermilion are natural, recyclable products made from wood grown
in sustainable forests.

A CIP catalogue record is available for this book from the British Library.

ISBN 9780091906740 (from January 2007)
ISBN 0091906741

Typeset by SX Composing DTP, Rayleigh, Essex
Printed and bound in Great Britain by Mackays of Chatham plc, Chatham, Kent

Contents

Introduction   1

1 Understanding Praise, and How Boys React to it   5

2 The Purpose of Praise   9

3 Keeping Praise Effective: Ten basic principles   32

4 Ages and Stages: Adapting to development   54

5 What to Notice and Encourage: Being creative   78

6 The Language of Praise: Ways to say it, and do it   100

7 Common Mistakes to Try to Avoid   122

8 Bribes, Rewards and Incentives   144

9 Using Praise to Encourage Learning and Behaviour   166

10 Avoiding the Perils of Perfectionism   190

11 Praise and You   212

Postscript   234

For Richard.
And with grateful thanks to all the young people
and adults who shared their stories with me.

Introduction

This book has been written for parents with boys of any age – babies, toddlers or teenagers – and for teachers. Most of the tips cover general principles that have broad application but several relate to the ages and stages of child development, acknowledging children's changing needs and perceptions. One of the most important lessons we have learnt over the last two to three decades is how much children, regardless of their age, benefit from receiving praise from parents and teachers. Children respond far better to positive feedback and encouragement than they do to threats, criticism and punishment. Many parents and teachers found it hard to use what they felt to be fulsome words, especially with boys; and although some still find it hard, most people are now sufficiently familiar and comfortable with common phrases to give praise in good measure.

Praise has been viewed as the way to boost children's self-esteem, to help them feel confident and to fulfil their potential and be at ease with themselves. Many won't realise that using praise also has wider benefits for individual children and society, because it can help to encourage self-discipline and moral behaviour. However, nothing about parenting or children is straightforward. Boys and girls, for example, often react to praise in different ways and need their confidence reinforced in different areas. We are also beginning to realise that if praise is over-used, used for particular personal motives or directed at the wrong kind of activity, it may actually be unhelpful. When praise is over-used, over-hyped or belies the truth, boys may either become praise dependent and require constant affirmation and approval, or become indifferent to it. Another possibility is that they may start to mistrust either the message or the messenger, wasting everyone's breath; or they might come to think they're super-clever and special and annoy people with their self-importance, when in truth they're simply normal. Boys in particular can also feel swamped and suffocated by what they can experience as a continuous positive or negative commentary on their every move and are inclined to act out to escape the microscopic attention and constant judgement.

In addition, there is growing concern that over-exposure to praise has led to children being ruined by rewards, dulled by 'dumbing down' and incapacitated by anxiety or, at the very least, easily wrong-footed when faced with real challenges. They may then hide their anxiety with diversionary displays of daring and bravado in other spheres. And there's the worry that boys are being softened by mollycoddling and lack the resilience valued in other societies. For praise to be reliably effective, we have to be careful and understand fully its pros and cons, wider value and the approaches that are safest given boys' particular sensitivities.

This is what this book sets out to achieve. The early chapters (1-6) present the basic principles, tactics and purposes. Chapter One develops an understanding of praise that underpins the thinking behind the 100 tips that are spread equally between the remaining ten chapters. Chapter Four enables readers to reflect upon the important features of child development and so relate the principles and tactics to the age and developmental stage of any particular boy. The later chapters (7-10) consider the subtleties and potential dangers of praise, and the final one invites the reader to self-reflect. Each tip stands alone and can be dipped into at random, but readers may like to read at least the introduction to each chapter in turn to gain an initial overview. It is a book to revisit on many occasions.

To offer a flavour of what this book will help you to understand, consider the following questions and try to spot the key differences between the possible responses:

When your son does particularly well, which might you say?
- I'm really proud of you for managing that!
- I hope you feel proud of yourself – you should.
- You probably feel really proud to have achieved that.
- I feel so proud of you and proud that you're my child.

If your son gets into the school football team, would you . . .?
- Say, Great! How many others tried for how many places?
- Promise to continue the trips to the pool to develop his skills further.

- Go as a family to every match to give him support.
- Attend yourself and shout encouragement from the sideline.

When your son tidies his room without being told, would you . . .?
- Give him a hug and bring him a hot or cold drink.
- Say thanks, but laugh and say you wonder how long it will last.
- Give him money, and hope this will persuade him to carry on the good work.
- Comment favourably on the improvement and ask what triggered the idea.

. . . Now read on!

CHAPTER 1

Understanding Praise, and How Boys React to it

Children love praise; of course they do, for most of us thrive on compliments and appreciation. Despite the pleasure it gives, children should be praised for more than just the delight it brings them or that it helps them try harder. Praise needs to be a central part of raising children because praise meets most of their fundamental needs. In other words, it is not merely a bit of luxury, some additional fancy wrapping that we can leave off if we prefer. Children need to feel important and significant to someone, to believe that someone cares enough to cherish them, and this is at least as important as being properly fed and clothed. Children need to feel secure and trust and rely on that care, which they can when they feel valued and central to their carer's life. They also need friendly and warm guidance, support and direction about how they should lead their lives, so they need to hear what it is they should do rather than how they constantly fall short and disappoint. And in order for children to flourish, they need to know and be told they are capable, are enjoyed and give pleasure – particularly to their parents.

Praise tends to be thought of as something spoken, put into words, but we can convey our pleasure, approval and appreciation in many ways. Hugs, smiles, rewards and touches, as we see in Chapter Six, all have their part to play and can sometimes be more effective because they can be more spontaneous and more direct. Even the spoken vocabulary of praise is more varied than at first appears, for the term 'praise' includes many types of phrase and expression that convey appreciation, acknowledgement or pure delight. The differences are important, as will become clear as the tips are explored.

It is deeply frustrating to realise that not all praise is helpful: just when we thought we were getting it right, people are saying we could be getting it wrong. The good news is that it is not complicated to work out which styles and phrases are likely to support achievement and which sentiments can become confusing or burdensome and could cause problems. Effective relationships are always those that manage to keep a range of needs, styles and goals in balance. The essence of constructive praise is that it is useful and encouraging: it provides relevant detailed information; it is believable so it is neither hollow nor false; and it may also show the way forward. Most important, the recipient should remain in full charge of his progress and be given opportunities to become confident in his ability to judge things for himself.

The energy that enables boys to take advantage of opportunity is self-belief. Self-belief is fuelled when boys genuinely feel capable because they know in detail what it was they did right (which means they know they can do it again), because they have acknowledged the mistakes they made in the past and now know how to avoid them (which means failures have been faced, not ignored) and because they feel certain that they are unconditionally loved and accepted for who they are, not for matching up to someone else's ideal or for something they're especially good at. It is rarely helpful to celebrate every success and ignore every failure. Just as certain types of praise can be unhelpful, criticism can be constructive – when mistakes are acknowledged, identified, ironed out and the necessary adjustments required made clear.

Boys do need to be affirmed and acknowledged as much as girls but given the culture amongst, especially older, boys, for being 'cool', not wanting to be considered a 'swot' and wishing to achieve without apparently trying, any praise or reward needs to be offered discreetly and with minimum fuss. Boys are not only readily embarrassed by overt praise (whether given in front of others or in private) but they are also more suspicious of it. They are more inclined to feel potentially manipulated by praise and to remain less seduced by it.

When given to older boys, praise needs to be either matter of fact – very descriptive of what has been achieved – or short. Young men tend to clothe themselves in confidence, sometimes to a degree that masks an underlying fear of failure. When boys fail to deliver what's expected, it is often because they have been cavalier about the amount of preparation that was necessary, have cut things too fine and aren't able to perform. In this event, the most useful response is to encourage them to look in detail at what they did not manage so they become clear what they need to do next time. They should not be allowed to hide behind some generalised assertion that it will be okay next time because they'll concentrate better, have a different teacher or start to knuckle down sooner.

Boys need to be overtly valued by adult males, their fathers especially. From the age of about eight, boys begin to dismiss girls and other females and increasingly challenge their mothers and female teachers as they explore their male identity and assert their masculinity. Female approval may become less valued for a while.

Boys of all ages, but particularly younger boys, find it quite hard to concentrate and apply themselves. 'Stickability' is their big weakness. They are very easily bored, diverted and distracted. In order to encourage boys to stay committed and focused, all positive feedback needs to be served up little and often but always discreetly. If we wait until the end of whatever it is they're supposed to be working on, it could be too late.

Boys need to be encouraged to become better organised, to plan ahead and may seem to need incentives and rewards to keep them focused. But being generally more attuned to power, boys are quick to bargain over the rewards offered and can twist them to their advantage. Boys will need to be encouraged and admired for their personal qualities that show caring and sharing, friendship and reliability, not simply for their strength or actions that ensure survival.

CHAPTER 2

The Purpose of Praise

What is praise for? It may seem an unnecessary question to ask but it is important to be clear about what it is we are trying to achieve in order to help us check whether what we say and do is all-round beneficial with no negative side effects. For example, parents of course want to help their sons grow up with good self-esteem. Self-esteem and strong self-belief are, indeed, valuable attributes, but their value is undermined if they come at the expense of sound self-knowledge (because they are told they're wonderful at everything), sound friendships (because friends are put off by the resulting bossiness and arrogance) and determination and perseverance (because they have never had to face and overcome setbacks). Praising certain reactions and behaviour can encourage the development of moral awareness by inviting children to reflect on their own behaviour and how they might change it and by commenting favourably on thoughtfulness; but if piling on praise leads to self-obsession and over-confidence, a boy's awareness of his impact on other people could be dulled. In order to decide whether our affirmative comments and actions are overall helpful, we should acknowledge the full range of possible desirable goals and the different categories and styles of positive feedback.

Here are some terms, all of which begin with the letter A, that help us to focus on the varied, deeper purposes of praise beyond the obvious ones.

Affirm; Appreciate; Approve; Admire; Attend; Anticipate; Achieve; Acknowledge; be Aware and Alert; Aspiration

Each of these ten simple objectives is explored as a separate tip in this chapter.

It is useful to consider praise in terms of time zones. Although each encounter and incident is in the present, a key purpose of praise – and of support and encouragement – is to help a boy feel optimistic about his future, comfortable with the route he has travelled from the past, as well as content with the present. When we *encourage* him, our focus is on the future – we try to convince any boy in our care he will overcome any current difficulty to be successful thereafter. We therefore generate faith, hope and confidence and give him heart. When we clearly *enjoy* his company and his achievements, we indicate our happiness and pleasure with who he is, in the present. When we *endorse* his actions, his view of the world, his approaches to learning and his feelings, we are accepting those bits of him that have been fashioned by his past. If boys are comfortable about past behaviour and experiences, even if these were difficult, they are better able to look optimistically at the future. It is not helpful for parents or significant others to make a boy feel either ashamed of or guilty about his past or to wipe it out in any attempt to refocus and start again.

1 Affirm – to help him feel strong

Q: *If parents don't praise you directly, how else might you know that they're pleased with you?*

A: *When they leave me alone and let me get on with things without nagging me. (16)*

A: *When they give me more responsibility, it shows they trust me. That gives me a buzz and is like praise. (15)*

To affirm a child is to make a clear statement that confirms and accepts who he is. The word has its origins in a Latin word that means strong. It therefore implies strength. When we affirm a child, we offer a firm statement of strong support, but it also gives children strength when they hear it.

To affirm is to make a neutral, judgement-free statement. Its essence is descriptive. The power and value of affirmation lies in its ability to encompass the past, present and future – to endorse and encourage. We do not have to wait for any particular event or achievement to speak out. We can help our son to understand who he is at any time by describing what we see – his qualities and personality, his likes and dislikes, his particular talents – and then confirm how much we enjoy and love him as he is.

Parents

* think of ways to describe how he is, thinks and does things that will 'firm him up', make him feel confident and strong inside:
- 'I love the way your eyes crinkle at the edges when you laugh'
- 'I've noticed how well you organise the football game in the park, which makes me think you're responsible enough to go into town with friends at the weekend'

* ask him to help you with tasks either because he is good company or because he's good at that sort of thing.

Teachers

* 'I like your ideas and what you are trying to say. They'd be clearer and more powerful if you separated them out. Try writing each idea down and thinking how they link to the rest'

* 'of course you will feel cross that Carl is using the computer before you, but alphabetical order is what the class agreed'

2 Appreciate his achievements

For a young child, every day brings fresh challenges and fresh achievements. One day he can't do something, yet the next he can. Life is a growing experience in which more becomes manageable so competence can blossom. These achievements become the expression of being and it is essential that they are fully appreciated.

One of the meanings of 'appreciate' is, be sensitive to. That is a significant definition. It suggests we should be sufficiently sensitive to see things on his level and in his terms: in relation to his challenges and difficulties, his limitations and capabilities, not our expectations.

'Appreciation' also covers the notion of value increasing, as in the value of houses or other forms of saving. Each child can be viewed as our most valuable asset. He will see that he goes up in your estimation each time you appreciate him and what he has managed to achieve. Of course you love him too, and he remains as important to you as ever, but every child really flies if he feels that those on whom he relies and whom he loves to the bottom of his being believe he has the potential to develop and impress.

Parents

- 'achievement' can be very widely interpreted: any advance in reading level, sociability, doing maths, height and reach, ball skills, being able to dress unaided, confidence, learning to swim, pack bags for school or an overnight with a friend, can be openly appreciated

- appreciation energises – when children hear your appreciation they feel able to move forward. Those who receive little can get emotionally and developmentally stuck and become demoralised

Teachers

- many schools have reward systems that acknowledge achievement for each individual, rather than what is exceptional for the group

- appreciate a wide variety of skills and knowledge, not simply those related to academic learning on which most lessons concentrate

3 Approve of who he is

Approval is the green light to grow, to carry on in the same way because he is good and lovely and fine as he is. Boys need this not only from their mothers, but also from their fathers, where this is practical or possible, or, if not, from an alternative father figure who knows him well and cares for his welfare. As soon as boys start to identify more closely with being male, from about the age of eight, they benefit from having an adult man available not just to approve of them but also to act as a positive role model as they explore ideas of masculinity and what it might mean for them. Male friends, uncles or cousins or a friendly neighbour may be able to step in where a father is not available. At the very least, mothers should be careful never to disparage men or men's characteristics in a boy's hearing, and they can help by speaking favourably of men in general or in particular wherever possible.

But gender is only one aspect of his identity – one of the later spoonfuls of colour added to his personality palette. He is already an individual and he needs to feel approved of for all his strengths, weaknesses, fears, habits and eccentricities.

Parents

- hear his side of the story; assume the best of him, not the worst

- let him tell you about his disappointments and realise what they mean to him

- respect his ideas – of what to play or wear; his methods – how to study; and his preferences when these are important

- listen to what he has to say, keeping your opinions to yourself unless he asks for them

Teachers

- avoid stereotyping – each boy is an individual, not a replica of anyone, even an older sibling

- acknowledge that each student's point of view will be the result of his unique experiences over the years

- accept that different children learn in different ways and be tolerant of each one's preferred style

4 Admire rather than adore

When parents put their sons on a pedestal, it presents them with a very hard act to follow. Most of them would prefer not to have that pressure. The following conversation between a mother and her two-year-old son highlights the problem. 'I adore you, Jamie!' 'Don't adore me, mummy.' 'Why not?' 'Because I cry too much.'

What Jamie was trying to say was: It is too much for me always to behave in a way that pleases you and makes you adore me. I know I'm not that good all the time, because I cry a lot which makes you cross and I can tell that you don't adore me then.

Adoration is a form of worship and children don't want to be treated as a god. We may feel it privately, for most of us think our children are heavenly, but we should express something more measured. We can admire how any boy in our care copes in a particular situation; admire how he manages to overcome his fears or admire how he approaches a problem. He will realise he is in command during these moments and the occasion is specific. What he certainly cannot directly control are our feelings: these are our business and it is unfair to load him with any responsibility for these. Even when he cries we should show we love him for being who he is.

Parents

- don't put him on a pedestal. Let him feel special to you because he is yours, but let him feel normal in relation to his peers

- show admiration for what he does: 'Well spotted', 'Nice work!', 'Great score line', but don't worship the ground he walks on

- keep him free of emotional obligations to you: don't require him to earn your love or behave so as to keep you entranced

Teachers

- teachers are unlikely to 'adore' a particular child in their class, but having one or two favourites is quite common. Boys in general feel uncomfortable being favoured – it marks them out when they'd prefer to be one of the lads

- try to keep even your admiration in proportion and always keep it private. Public accolades for creditable work can lead to teasing about being teacher's pet. For example, have a quick word as he leaves the classroom or if you use email at school, send a brief message

5 Attention is what all boys really want

I hate it when adults ignore me! It makes me feel like an ant. (10)

Children need to be noticed. They are very small creatures in a very big world which is sure to appear huge, confusing and even intimidating to them. Our supportive attention fires them up; it gives them the energy and confidence to find their way. Without it, they can feel lost and as small and insignificant as an ant.

Boys also need appreciative attention. When boys are young, they are learning at a speed that would exhaust most adults. What gives them special pleasure is to gain greater control of their bodies and their life as they become taller, stronger and better coordinated. They can acquire an enormous sense of pride in their achievements as they reach the top of the climbing frame, learn to jump in the deep end of the swimming pool, manage stunts on their bikes or simply become sufficiently tall to open the freezer or reach the tap or light switch. At these moments of personal triumph, their whole self shouts 'look at me!' If we are absent in either body or mind, they could become dejected and crestfallen.

Parents

* remember that attention-seeking is usually attention-needing. Give him more attention if he starts to pester and irritate, but only once he has calmed down

* when you are focusing on him, give him your full attention: don't answer the telephone; don't tuck in a coffee with a friend on your special trip out; and refer to any special chats or episodes later, so he knows you logged them

* think of the everyday things you do that he might feel excluded from and ways he could become more involved; for example, could you show him your workplace?

Teachers

* identify the boys you have contact with who are quiet or withdrawn or who have 'gone off the boil' and make a point of speaking briefly to each of them after the lesson or around school several times over the next three to four weeks

* if a quiet boy is with friends when you pass, you may decide to leave it; alternatively you could ask if he has a moment to discuss something and try to include a practical issue as well as something affirming so he can provide a safe answer to his friends if they ask him what you want

* just a smile and a 'How's things?' could be enough

6 Anticipate his problems and feelings

Boys, more so than girls, live in the here and now. They act and quickly react, want to get things done and over with and then move on. They are less inclined to think ahead to the possible consequences of any of their actions and are therefore more likely to find themselves in trouble. Boys also tend to blank out thoughts about things they'd rather weren't happening, or wish did not have to happen, such as bedroom tidying, packing for a holiday or exam revision, and rely instead on their belief that they will cope when they have to. But boys need to become more mindful of the future – delightful though their energetic, youthful spontaneity is – because they need to learn to plan, anticipate, be careful and caring and take responsibility.

Demonstrate by example and try to anticipate how a boy may respond to something potentially difficult that is coming up in order to help him prepare. Encourage him to be honest about and reflect on his feelings by chatting about how you felt when it happened to you, or say, 'I imagine that was/could be difficult for you.' Although we would not want to generate anxiety where none existed, boys can be relieved to discover someone understands any, often heavily disguised, worry.

Parents

• anticipate how he might react to something that is about to happen. If he is distressed or disappointed, tell him you realise that and address the details that may worry him to put him more at ease. He will at least feel accepted and understood

• through positive feedback and prompting, lots of talk that focuses on today's, yesterday's and tomorrow's events, we can help him anticipate outcomes and become more sensitive to other people's likely reactions

• rather than allow him to stay safe in the present, help him to reflect on the past and future and make sense of these if they are uncomfortable

Teachers

• try to imagine the particular difficulty a boy who is struggling might confront with a particular assignment. Approach him and acknowledge this, perhaps suggesting a few helpful guidelines

• give him faith in his ability to do the assignment well enough, in a way that represents a learning advance for him

7 Help him achieve his aims

Aged 10, my son decided he wanted to undertake a detailed nature survey of the local park. He was passionate about small creatures and wanted to lay small mammal traps to do a count, as well as search for beetles and other insects. I took him to the nearest specialist map shop and bought a large scale map of the area. Then I helped him to rule lines on it to divide it into smaller squares. He started to dig about and record his findings but couldn't keep it up. It was too big a project. But at least he realised I respected his dreams and how you can make something happen.

Boys are inclined to lose heart and direction easily. While they may resent interference, they generally appreciate receiving help to stay on track where a task becomes tedious or to bring any fanciful ideas to fruition when their imagination takes off.

Without getting pushy or demanding, adults can help boys achieve their dreams. We can shore up their faith in themselves and teach them how to translate often elaborate ideas into practical action.

Parents

* whereas it may be pushy to ensure boys reach the goals we determine, it is wholly supportive and encouraging when we help him identify practical pathways to those he sets for himself

* help him to set out a detailed plan that will enable him to achieve his more challenging aspirations

* ask him what equipment or help he needs, but don't take it over and make it your project

Teachers

* it is important that children receive constructive feedback that helps them to learn, develop their understanding and, through this process, increasingly learn how to manage their own progress

* boys will be helped to achieve their aims when they are actively involved in planning their work, then carry out their plan, ending with a review of what went right and wrong in order to assess how to approach that same task next time. This is known as 'feedback for learning'; in shorthand, plan, do, review, then reframe the task

8 Acknowledge his personal strengths

Boys don't have to be 'good at' something before they gain our attention and regard. Each will possess personal qualities, inclinations, interests and strengths that can be noted, appreciated and – most importantly – brought to his attention. Praise should always encompass far more than pats on the back for specific accomplishments. If we reflect back and give a name to some of the warmer, caring qualities he demonstrates to his brothers and sisters, to us or to his friends, as well as to those strengths such as perseverance or determination that encourage achievement, he will be able to develop a picture of his whole self just as he can see his physical self in a mirror. It will help him to become more aware of his social qualities and consider these important too.

The kinds of personal strengths we can acknowledge and name include thoughtfulness, understanding, good at sharing, caring, forthrightness, curiosity, sense of humour, good memory, well-organised, imaginative, able to relax, carefree, good powers of concentration, interested in ideas and well-coordinated.

Parents

* acknowledge the full range of possible talents and interests

* acknowledge positive thoughts as well as well as positive deeds

* focus on the necessary 'doing' aspects of achievement – the inclination to try – as well as the amount he tried by the end of the process

Teachers

* acknowledge that each child is an individual with rights to be heard and respected

* list the personal strengths of any boy whose behaviour is causing concern and make sure he and other children realise you appreciate these

* choose him to perform any task that might use or develop his personal strengths

* take care to balance out your attention sufficiently so an attempt to help one individual does not come across as favouritism

9 Be aware and alert

We cannot talk about what we have noticed unless we remain aware of his moods, what has delighted him, his preferences and so on. We can be with our child all day without really noticing any of these, or we can see our son for only two or three hours a day and be acutely sensitive to his body language, expressions, tone of voice, choices and demeanour.

Being aware does not necessarily mean we should discuss every concern or interpretation then and there but we would be wise to note it and watch for a possible pattern. For boys especially, too much expressed 'sensitivity' can feel intrusive. 'Stop trying to get inside my head!' was one eleven-year-old's frustrated cry to his mother when she was trying hard to be empathic. Especially after a tiring day at school, boys want to relax, remain quiet and reflect. Any rebuff, often indicated by a curt 'fine', is not necessarily a sign of big trouble he'd rather keep private, just the need to be quiet and alone for a while.

Parents

- watch discreetly how he relates to his brothers and sisters; compliment him if he is helpful, kind and caring or if he manages to ignore being baited by others

- make a mental note of which events enthuse him and which tend to make him sad or disappointed

- be careful not to seem like a spy: 'I have generally noticed / been aware / It's become clear to me that . . .' is better than, 'I have been watching you from a distance and I've seen you be really . . .'

- if something important is to happen at school – a test, a notable visitor, a special fun class, a class play – ensure you remember to ask how it went

Teachers

- it is easy to comment positively on students' work when they hand it in as an assignment but less easy to remark on their wider attitudes and supportive behaviour unless you look out for these

- be alert for signs of sadness or depression; a sensitivity to these will imply you have bothered to notice and know him well enough to realise things aren't quite right

10 His, not your, aspirations matter most

I've already decided. He's going to be a doctor when he grows up. I've set my heart on it and I'm going to do everything I can to get him interested in human biology and how the body works as he goes through school!

This single mum had had a hard time and was desperate to give her son a better life. She thought that giving him clear aspirations for a stable and successful professional future would be the best she could do for him. Her son is still too young to know whether she will get her way! While it is certainly better that we look hopefully on his future prospects rather than professing doubt and derision, it is, though, potentially dangerous to be as pre-determined as this mum.

She may, for example, stifle some special interest that develops for fear it could divert him from her chosen path. Her dreams may become obvious and he may be tempted to thwart her from spite. He may, though, enjoy following this destiny and see it as a gently amusing game. The most valuable thing we can nurture in any boy is the confidence, optimism, trust, motivation, space and self-determination to develop his own aspirations.

Parents

* offer plenty of attention, affirmation and structure so he has the confidence to imagine himself doing well and the creativity to aspire

* help to ground those aspirations in reality by discussing practical plans for making them happen

* even small boys will express wishes and desires: 'I want to draw a plan of the back garden', 'I'd like to play a Star Wars™ game when Sam comes over', 'I'd like to play the guitar'. If you help to make these happen, he will know it is safe to dream and possible to influence his destiny

* help to make his future feel safe and full of potential by creating a secure present

Teachers

* learning should help us all to explore 'our possible selves'. It should open up possibilities not close them down

* help boys to express their aspirations. After a good piece of work or a good term, ask where he sees this leading or what he has in mind for his future because you see a rosy one

* from a young age, boys can be encouraged to consider the future and imagine where they see themselves, in terms of jobs, family situation and pastimes and where they might live. Any fanciful answers can be prompted with, 'That's great! Now your task is to plan how you can make this happen'

CHAPTER 3

Keeping Praise Effective: Ten basic principles

Keeping praise effective is important. There is no point praising a boy if he is going to end up feeling oppressed or manipulated by it or resentful because we have not got it right. Resentful children have a tendency to hit back where it hurts most, so if we show that his performance on the soccer pitch or baseball field, in school or on the stage is the part of him that really matters to us, that could be what he decides to opt out of either to pay us back for our interference or to deflect the constant pressure.

We praise children because we believe it helps them, so there is no point, either, in trying to build a child's confidence if it leads to the opposite: a child with an uncertain sense of self-worth who needs constant reinforcement and continuous success to remain convinced of his ability and our approval. It is not good when a boy becomes so used to praise that its absence implies disapproval or disappointment. It seems a tricky path to tread, but it is not difficult if the principles of effective praise are followed.

The hallmarks of constructive praise are that it should:

- *strengthen self-belief*, so it should generalise the achievement and pay as much attention to his capacity to achieve as to the specific outcome. Possible comments are, 'You're good at *that sort of thing*' or, 'Now you've done it once, that should give you the confidence to understand it next time and thereafter'.
- *be useful because it shows the way forward.*
- *leave him with the possibility and opportunity to change*, be different or to do something differently next time. It should not, therefore, lock any boy into a single way to please, perform or do things by being too narrow and focused. Children develop and change as they mature and grow, as adults do, which is one of the potential delights of living for all of us.
- *avoid dependency*, by encouraging him gradually to judge things for himself, and making clear your confidence in his ability to do so. It will also help him to realise that what matters most is the pattern of his personal progress and learning, not the precise outcome on any specific occasion.

11 Let him impress you

Boys love it when someone they respect and admire shows clearly and freely they are genuinely impressed by something they have done. Showing and stating you are impressed is a very effective and straightforward form of praise, which helps them to stand taller, inspired by extra confidence and pleasure.

Being impressed sidesteps the judgement that is implied in so much praise. Most important, it is unconditional. 'I am really impressed!' or 'That was impressive!' says it all – no ifs and buts to qualify or detract from the message. There is nothing grudging about being impressed and when boys hear it they are able to feel top dog.

Fathers who are able to be impressed with their sons clear the air of competition. It levels the playing field, for it shows you don't need to prove that you are stronger, better and more clever. And being impressed doesn't mean a boy has 'won' in some way or will stop trying. It simply signifies respect and admiration, which is what boys thirst for.

Parents

- compare him favourably with you as a child: 'I couldn't have managed that when I was your age', 'I wish I'd been able to do/draw/sing as well as you can'

- 'I thought you played impressively well. Were you pleased with what you did?'

- when playing any game, let a little one win in little ways, and show you're impressed with his increasing skill

- ask him to help you fix things, organise things, decide things, clean things then say, 'Wow, you're ace at that, aren't you?'

Teachers

- 'you showed an impressive degree of understanding in that essay'

- 'I'm impressed that this piece of work was so much better laid out. It must have taken you longer, but thanks for giving it extra time'

- 'that's an impressive improvement. Well done!'

- give boys responsibilities, such as reporting back on group discussions and looking up information for everyone's benefit; show how impressed you are with the outcome

12 Make it mean something – be specific

It helps boys to feel comfortable about accepting praise if it is descriptive and specific: related to a particular piece of work, achievement or action and to a particular aspect of it. Of course, describing something in detail proves without doubt you have noticed your son's effort or thoughtfulness, but your observations also help the feedback to be accurate and relevant while having the additional advantage of avoiding being judgemental.

Boys, though, also benefit from being open about mistakes. This is because their natural cockiness, that may shade into over-confidence, can predispose them to deny that there is more to learn. They're more likely to claim they did well because they're 'good' at something, than because they practised in a particular way, had developed good memory techniques or had finally understood something. Similarly, they're inclined to claim they did badly because they did not train or revise properly, because the test or competition was stupid or the teacher was inept. Offering detail will help to convince your son that he understands what he's doing right and can repeat it. Misplaced confidence may sometimes get boys out of a hard place, but it doesn't help anyone who needs to make solid progress step by step.

Parents

• describe in some detail what he's done that is pleasing so he's clear what's right about his approach and what he needs to repeat next time

• with a model or painting, discuss the colours used or the size or shape. Ask why or whether he likes what he's done, whether he planned it or it just turned out that way

• describe what you appreciated about how he behaved after the event rather than comment every few minutes as the occasion unfolds

Teachers

• encourage boys to evaluate each other's work having discussed as a class important points to watch out for

• boys need to know in detail what they did right and wrong so comments and marks should be full and clear at the same time as encouraging

• help him to feel it is okay to be proud of good work. 'I bet you felt pretty happy with this piece of work. You should have done'

13 Keep praise private

I don't mind a teacher saying something like, 'Well done' or 'I liked this' when he hands back work in class but it totally freaks you out if he goes on and on about how good it was. It's so embarrassing! I quite like it when it's given as part of the team effort – you know: the football team did well in their league match, and Gerry Thomas got four of the five goals, but if it was 'Gerry Thomas was the star of the match. He held it altogether . . .', that's not so good. (15)

As boys grow older, and especially when they get to secondary school or college, praise given in public, even in front of the class, tends to make them squirm. They are not sure how to react to it when there are rows of friends' and enemies' faces in front of them because it is probably not acceptable to admit to and show they are pleased; and they do not want anyone to think that they've worked hard enough to get the attention of the teacher, who may not in any case be liked by everyone.

It's easier at home, but even then everyday praise should be a private matter between parent and son, not paraded as something for any siblings to get jealous about.

Parents

- celebration is a public statement, but everyday praise should be private

- ask yourself whose business this is. Usually, it relates only to parent and child, for it is no one else's responsibility

- keeping praise private helps to keep it in proportion. The more people you tell, or the more people are present when you say it to him, the more it will seem to grow in importance and have unintended consequences

Teachers

- private praise helps to focus him safely on his personal progress. Public praise may encourage unhelpful competition and may lead boys to work for the wrong reasons

- don't assume all boys want public recognition in, for example, assemblies; some may under perform to avoid being accused of being a swot

- send parents a note detailing the improvement; most boys would prefer parents to know than classmates

- have a quiet word with a pupil as he leaves the class if you want to say a special well done

14 Let him take all the credit

It is often taken as a sign of good teaching or parenting if a child excels, so either adult may seek to claim credit when a pupil, son or class does well. Of course we might have had some influence, by reading to him a great deal when he was young, driving him to and from extra classes or training, helping him with his maths when stuck, encouraging him to keep a daily diary on special holidays or nurturing any special fascination with insects, electronics or dinosaurs that might have livened his mind. But his actual achievement – on the day – is always his and it is cruel, selfish and short-sighted to suggest anything else. If we need to boost our own self-esteem through claiming success on the back of our child's, the most obvious message is that success is something he, too, needs before he can feel acceptable and complete.

In the same vein, if we help in a manner that makes him believe – or means he cannot be sure – that his success was down to us not him, it dilutes the potential gain in self-belief and confidence, which would be a great pity if he could have achieved it on his own.

Parents

* never attribute any of his success to you. Make it clear that he can feel one hundred per cent it was his work; otherwise, he may feel he needs you next time too

* if you find yourself saying, 'That homework we did . . . What was our mark?', realise that you could be about to walk off not only with some of the credit but also with ownership of the work!

* if he mentions your help, restate it was he who delivered on the day, and further help won't be necessary

Teachers

* in the context of league tables, it is hard not to claim much of the credit if a whole class does better than expected. Nevertheless, each child must feel he did it himself, even if he was well-taught by you!

* the more detail a boy has about why he did well, the more he can see and believe it was his knowledge, learning and application that took him there

15 Be careful with judgement

My friend was very keen on manners. Her little boy had to be polite and aware of others at all times, even though he was only five or six. He was praised well for this. But if he bumped into someone while walking down the street, dropped a sweet wrapper or didn't think to step aside for a pushchair, he was reprimanded for his disappointing behaviour. He couldn't cope with being judged for things he was too young to control and at home he regressed, ending up wanting to be bottle-fed like his baby sister.

Children need to be noticed rather than judged. It is fine to evaluate some of what they do but it is not fine to be judgemental about who they are. When children are young they cannot conceptualise this distinction. They don't want to be monitored and evaluated from dawn to dusk, bearing the burden of always being watched and having to stay in line. Expectations must always be appropriate and evaluative praise reserved for actions that boys can easily change. Children thrive when they are open and feel free within safe limits, not where they are constantly looking over their shoulder or anticipating good or bad remarks.

Parents

*   make sure your expectations are age appropriate. Boisterous boys can be enthusiastic rather than thoughtless, careless or determinedly naughty

*   keep shame and guilt out of it, at least until he is about ten years old when he has the capacity to control and self monitor and can clearly separate what he does from who he is

*   you bring about what you fear. Many boys will flaunt bad behaviour if they are endlessly told off. It ends the waiting and puts them in control so is less humiliating

Teachers

*   encourage boys to assess their own work

*   keep feedback neutral and descriptive rather than either fulsome or disappointed

*   shame often encourages boys to ignore or reject suggestions for improvement; use it very sparingly

16 Be truthful, not gushing

Boys don't feel comfortable with what they might view as 'gush and mush' – over-enthusiastic adulation that seems unrelated to the effort that was entailed and was certainly not expected, let alone desired. It is too emotional, too intimate and encourages them to believe that they are responsible for a parent's excessive delight and it's the parent's delight that counts. What counts, of course, is their own sense of pride, fulfilment and pleasure – they must eventually do things to a standard to please themselves, not to gain riotous applause from the parental gallery.

False praise is not only offensive and insulting; it also does not help boys to develop good judgement. Over time, they must learn to judge their effort and work for themselves. If we go overboard when they know something could have been done better, they will find it harder to tell what is good enough and what could be improved upon. Boys tend naturally to over-value their work. Gushing adds to that unhelpful tendency.

Parents

* don't pretend, but be positive and upbeat where you can. Make the scope for improvement very clear and encourage him to accept and understand shortcomings. 'I don't quite call this a tidied room. You've done well so far but that pile of comics still needs to be sorted. When you've finished, I'll bring you up a drink and admire it!'

* focus on the pleasure he gets, so he learns to perform to for his gain, not yours

Teachers

* some children need more of a boost and find measured praise hard to believe. However, these boys just need it said more often, not more enthusiastically or exaggeratedly, because they won't believe that either

* if you are honest but encouraging about the bad, students will be more inclined to believe honestly-given praise

17 Praise the process not the product

Many sceptics of the value of praise complain that the quality of the product does matter, and more than the process. What is the point, they argue, in claiming something is good when it is not, and with ignoring the explanation – that someone simply did not try hard enough when they could obviously do better?

Naturally, at some point the quality does matter and boys should, indeed, be called to account for behaviour or performance that suggests inadequate attention. However, the sceptics misunderstand the advice: trying is always valuable, for no one makes any progress without some commitment and effort applied to learning more or doing better. Effort involves skills such as determination and tenacity that need to be valued and encouraged. At the beginning of any new challenge, effort is necessarily crude and inefficient, but that is the route all of us took and we came through. In addition, what younger boys produce is always flawed compared with what we could do and they cannot continuously be told something is not good enough.

Parents

* as 'process' includes keenness, application, determination and good work habits, these attributes should be valued as part of learning and growing

* if your son's school supplies a separate effort mark that measures how hard he tried, take this seriously. It will be sensitive to his age and stage

* young children don't understand what it means to try hard or concentrate. Encourage this by reading through longer stories or playing board games that take time, patience and thought

* learning is an emotional process, so ask if it was hard, if he worried about the outcome or if he faltered in the middle

Teachers

* through use of the 'plan, do, review' model of learning (see page 25), children can begin to reflect on their working style and learn to judge the effectiveness of their efforts

18 Tell it straight and straight away

For best effect, praise should be given straight, with no ifs and buts, no sarcasm, no reminders of past failures or other put downs to dilute its effect.

And it should be given straight away wherever possible as that conveys spontaneity. Sometimes the positive response does not occur to us at the time, or we are busy with other children so don't really take the relevant information in. A parent who is away for work should be primed to say something appreciative on the telephone that day rather than wait until the homecoming and receive the lists of good deeds that need complimenting. As boys are embarrassed by overt and public praise, they would rather hear an informal, more natural comment at the time even if that means it is less well-informed than a measured, serious assessment delivered later.

Better late than never is certainly advisable; but even better to say it sooner rather than later.

Parents

- children take praise very seriously so treat it seriously. It's not the moment for jokes so don't be sarcastic if you want your comments to be effective

- if you didn't respond at the time, make amends by saying something like, 'I thought again about what you told me, properly this time. Sounds like you did really well and it was important. That's terrific'

- say it like you mean it: while you are looking at your child, not as you turn to leave the room

Teachers

- the quicker you can give feedback on work done, the more a boy will learn from your comments because he will still remember how he approached the task

- if you make positive comments on children's personalities, interests, sociability and style, these can be given straight away

19 Focus on the achievement, rather than on him

'Focus on the behaviour, not the child' is recommended by most parenting pundits. It is fundamental, and as relevant to giving praise as to meting out discipline and punishment when the golden rule is usually promoted. Separating children from their behaviour makes so much sense in relation to discipline. Letting a child know he's loved – that we're just not wild about what he's done – allows every child to hold on to that all-important sense of self-worth that feeds self-respect and the will to do well.

In relation to praise, we should always focus on what it is our son has achieved, not on who he is. 'That was terrific, what you managed to do' is a far less emotionally entangling thing to say than 'You're so wonderful to have got that far / done that. I love you so much!' He may not feel so wonderful, knowing full well he didn't pull out all the stops for this event. He may realise, too, that you tell him off when he has been naughty so he knows he is not always so wonderful. We should love and feel proud of our boys all the time, not only when they have done well.

Parents

* boys under three cannot separate what they do from who they are, so very young boys need it very simple. Approval words that mention the achievement will be enough, such as 'Well tried!', 'Eating all your dinner was great', 'Great catch!', 'Lovely picture', 'Good boy to wait your turn'

* from about aged ten, boys feel more emotionally independent. They no longer want lashings of loving stuff because they are trying to be free. Surprise hugs are great, but praise should always commend the achievement, not him. 'That was a clever thing to do' not, 'You are so clever'

Teachers

* boys may like to feel liked, as in accepted and enjoyed, by their teachers but they tend not to relish favouritism or personal comments. 'John always gives his work in on time' is easier to accept than 'John's the only reliable boy here when it comes to handing in work'

* 'that exercise you did for me last month was great. That shows you can do it', rather than 'You're a clever boy, if only you'd believe it. Of course you'll do it fine'

20 Ask him how he wants it

After football on a Saturday my twelve-year-old son often asks me how I thought he played and I reply, 'How do you want it?' We have this scheme: he can ask for it 'straight', 'gentle', or 'I'll guess what you think'. If he's feeling up to an honest account that he thinks ought to be critical, he'll say, 'straight'.

There are two parties in any learning situation – the teller and the person being told. To be effective as a mentor, coach or mere supporter, we have to understand how the information could be received. Truth and honesty may be what we're ready to give, but if the boy who receives the 'telling' isn't ready to hear that, he can block it by denying or ignoring it.

So if we decide the time has come not to beat about the bush any more, either because he's now older and may not need so much cushioning or because he has started to misjudge himself, we can begin by giving him some control over the level of honesty in any feedback. If we give him the choice of hearing the good news or the bad news first, he's far more likely to remain receptive.

Parents

• be sensitive to the moment: consider the context and recent events. If he's had a tough time and disappointments elsewhere, don't choose that moment to 'give it to him straight'!

• if you have not put the question back to him and asked him what he thinks, begin your reply, '*I think you know this already* . . . you were a bit slow off the mark at the start / you weren't turning quickly enough . . .' The point is to encourage him to have faith in his own assessment, not become dependent on you

• always ask at the end, 'Did you think my comment was fair?'

Teachers

• check afterwards how your comment was received. 'I was quite honest with you on that. Did it upset you or was it helpful?'

• feedback is a process and learning is two-way. Allow and encourage students to reflect and discuss with you how they react to your style and approach. Take class soundings but note individuals' views too

CHAPTER FOUR

Ages and Stages: Adapting to development

The five separate stages of childhood mark out key changes in children's needs, in what they are progressively able to do, how they are able to think, what they are able to understand and therefore in how they will to see themselves. It is clear, then, that parents and teachers need to be sensitive to these changes and adjust their praise style and strategies as boys mature.

Newborn babies are engrossed with their physical needs and very dependent for these on their carer. But they also respond vigorously to close attention and react to it very physically – every bit of their body moves and their whole being seems engaged in the communication. Baby boys are particularly active: they move more than girls inside the womb and they are more energetic after they are born. Newborn babies have to face a bewildering array of sounds, smells, signs and behaviours. The challenge for carers is to make them feel physically and emotionally safe through establishing reliable close contact and familiarity through regular routines and patterns.

Sometime during their second year, the baby becomes a walking and talking toddler. These skills make him feel far more independent and his sense of self becomes clearly established. He will want to explore, experiment and examine everything. Though he's now capable of doing so much more, the overwhelming experience for a boy can be one of failure and incompetence as he stumbles and fumbles, breaks things, misjudges things and tries to make sense of the myriad rules that suddenly appear. At this age, boys are generally less well coordinated than girls, far clumsier and less able to explain themselves. What toddlers need from parents and carers keen to nurture self-esteem is a great deal of tolerance of the genuine and inevitable mistakes made during the steepest learning curve of his life. Plenty of encouragement for each small step made towards self-management and self-control, tolerance of his frustrations and lots of attention will help him to feel noticed, competent, understood and affirmed.

From the age of four to about seven, boys see life very simply: things are either good or bad or right or wrong, which also means that they see themselves in the same simple terms, as either a good boy or a bad boy. Subtlety is not what they're about or what they see, so parents should think carefully about the balance of positive and negative feedback they give. Most of the time these school-age children want to please, provided they're not angry about feeling left out or being unloved. They still rely on copying – parents, brothers and sisters – for a lot of their learning, and they need signs of approval that they're on the right track.

In the pre-teen years, boys may become more suspicious of parents' use of praise or simply get bored with trying to please: they would prefer to get on with life and not be on constant watch for an adult's pleasure or disappointment. Tweens are starting to separate, especially from their mothers, are enjoying their growing freedom and paying increasing attention to the views of friends. However, they need lots of positive back-up as they try out a broader range of skills and activities that their stronger bodies allow. At this stage, appreciation for what they can now do is at least as important as approval for who they are. Sibling rivalry could begin to focus on competing talents, so make sure all children feel equally loved and accepted despite varying abilities and aptitudes.

Teenage boys still like to be praised, but if it goes over the top they feel uncomfortable. They enjoy their efforts being noticed and appreciated but they are beginning to judge much more for themselves and know exactly how big a deal any achievement is. As one fifteen-year-old boy said, 'My father doesn't praise me as much, so when it comes from him I get more of a rush and I feel good. It feels like it's really worthwhile.' Another said, 'As you get older you don't expect it so much. You're more independent. It gets more patronising when it's too frequent.' One issue with teenage boys is that their increasing independence makes it harder to know what they're doing, good or bad. Any inquisition is likely to feel intrusive and make them turn hoof. Their very need for more privacy suggests they want parents less and more time alone to work things out for themselves. So lie low, save your celebrations for the notable successes and in the meantime, focus on affirmation. Make sure, too, you don't criticise their views and values, their friends, ideas, clothes, passions or their creativity, all of which are essential parts of their maturing identity.

21 Make babies feel safe and secure

Babies are able to read people long before they can read words. They notice and recognise our moods, tone of voice and physical movements long before they can understand what is being said. They will be more sensitive to these than possibly at any other time of their lives, as it is through recognising patterns in these that they feel linked to our world. Almost from the moment of birth we know they copy as a way to communicate because they can poke out the tip of their tongue when someone does it to them at close range. They let us know how they feel through their limbs that either flail in distress or twitch excitedly; and, of course, through crying and smiling. Their cries can express hunger, discomfort, loneliness, boredom or anxiety – any of which an adult might feel. By meeting their need for food, safety, love, warmth and security, we demonstrate that we understand them and their need for us, which is sufficiently affirming to them that we can call it praise. What matters to them is less *what* we say than that we say, or even sing, something to them in tones that are familiar and sound soothing. Simply talking, even out of view, tells them that we are near. Paying closer attention shows that we care and they can rely on us.

Parents

* at this age, attention-seeking is definitely attention-needing. Babies become distressed when someone who is playing with them looks or moves away; and they come alive when we connect with them directly

* choose a song to sing at each clear stage of their day: to mark feeding, bath time or nappy changing, for example. He will then begin to recognise the tunes and predict the day's regular routines

* holding and carrying him, playing with his nose or chin, fingers and toes establishes and helps him to experience his physical boundary, which gives him his first sense of self

Teachers/carers

* one-to-one contact with young babies is very important to ground their sense of being, safety and significance

* regular and reciprocal social, visual and emotional contact and stimulation helps their newly formed brains to establish positive neural connections

* routines are vital to give any baby or young child a sense of safety, order and security

22 Babies must feel they're important

As far as anyone can tell, new babies have very little awareness of having a separate identity: they merge with their care giver as one. One key way in which they begin to realise they develop that sense of being a significant, important and separate person is to have us be in tune with them and responsive to the signals they send out. Psychologists call this form of give and take, notice and react, style of interacting 'synchronicity' and 'reciprocity'. It is comforting for babies, even at this level, to know that they can communicate, be heard and understood. This is a far cry from the scheduled, over-organised, packaged up and packed off babies that are required to fit in to other people's superimposed and fixed routines – though it has already been said they need some routine. To reciprocate implies respect for the growing person and his developing personality. This requires that we look, listen and notice, respond and love and care.

Parents

- allow him to develop his own patterns and pace, and respect these

- babies work very hard to form an intimate relationship with their care giver. If we fail to notice their efforts and ignore them, they will then stop trying and switch off

- playing with his fingers, face and toes; holding him tight and sharing with him the rhythm of our body, as he shares his with us; and responding to his fears, delights and sufficiency in relation to food, sleep or entertainment, tells him of our deep sense of love and regard for his being and welfare

Teachers/carers

- endeavour to maintain a carer-infant ratio that enables individual infants' patterns to be respected, within a structure that offers familiarity and security

- professional convenience matters, but not if it is acquired at the expense of infant health and contentedness

23 Give your toddler a positive view of himself

Toddlers have a hard time because they make lots of mistakes and are very accident-prone. They can irritate their parents sometimes beyond measure as they try to carve out space for themselves and strive to be listened to in a family's otherwise busy life. Living with a toddler can be a constant battle, and if it is, it can be well nigh impossible to say enough positive, affirmative, approving and appreciative things to offset the negative signals we send through shouting, anger, frustration or simply insisting that our will be done. Yet toddlers need to feel loved and successful to thrive, just like older boys.

Even during the 'terrible twos', a boy will not yet have a clear sense of his unique self. He is as he does. When we reprimand him for what he does, applying the behaviour/self rule in order to protect his self-respect, he may still feel personally at fault because he is too young to sense or comprehend the difference.

Physical affirmation – that is, plenty of cuddles and close physical contact – will help him get the simple yet strong message that we continue to love and approve of him despite the hassles.

Parents

* give him plenty of cuddles and physical reassurance, especially after a 'bad patch'. Don't necessarily talk, or just say 'That was a tough day!'

* make a joke to end the arguing: 'How silly we are, fighting like a cat and dog!'

* toddlers experience themselves through action. Encourage self-management in as many tasks as possible to help a growing boy feel positive about his role in your world

* encourage him to dress himself – even if the socks are odd, the T-shirt back to front or colours clash! Involve him in tasks that don't require perfection, such as digging the garden or decorating biscuits

Teachers/carers

* listening helps boys to feel they matter. Ensure each boy has someone who has time to hear his point of view

* when small children are herded, they may feel very insignificant

* behaviour talks: what is he saying? Get to the bottom of persistent bad behaviour quickly, before he becomes sure he is a bad boy

24 Tolerate your toddler's frustrations

Until the age of eighteen months, Jack was a model baby. Then, like a typical toddler, he became defiant and disobedient and hated being told no. Jack often flung himself on the floor, kicking and screaming; he would refuse to get out of his car seat; scream if I got his drink wrong, in the supermarket or when I tried to get him dressed ready to go to my mum's. Then I decided to pay him more attention, not be so strict, let him decide little things and to play with him more. The improvement was dramatic.

Toddlers are trying because they're trying it on – almost all the time. Having been carried, sat, fed, dressed, driven and otherwise 'done to' all their short life, they have learned they can be a force to be reckoned with. Toddlers use their expanding vocabulary, stronger bodies and clearer sense of self and purpose to say no and assert themselves – it's an intoxicating power that they use to get noticed, gain some control and feel important.

But toddlers also struggle with frustration because they can still achieve so little. Their ideas race ahead of their bodies and they confront real rules. He feels more grown up, yet he still can't master every task or express complex and powerful feelings.

Parents

• don't take it personally. He does not hate you or want to get at you – he's just expressing complex and powerful feelings he can't put into words

• express his frustrations for him. 'It must have been hard, being ignored / wanting me to stay with you when I had to leave / being fed up with being told what to do and when to do it, when you felt like staying at home and playing'

• explain to his older brothers or sisters why he feels so frustrated and why that can make him a nuisance to them

• make it clear whenever you can that you know he's not being bad, just finding life hard at the moment

Teachers/carers

• offer chances for boys to play through their frustrations

• choose stories to read that represent their difficulties, so they know they're not alone and feel more understood

25 Understand what a schoolboy can't understand

Most arguments between parents and children happen when children fail to match up to parental expectations. Older children may choose to play in a pop band rather than follow mum or dad into the favoured family profession, but clashes with young children usually occur where a child cannot think or behave in the way his parents expect, when he is consequently considered thoughtless, selfish, immature or even spiteful.

Boys aged between four and seven or eight are not, and cannot be, grown up. Children develop slowly and in set ways, and boys are often slower developers than girls. 'Don't be such a baby!' is especially humiliating when thrown at boys who will have already picked up that they should be more resilient, reliable, organised, cooperative and less emotional than they are capable of being. Praise should not be conditional on him understanding more than he can. And criticism should not fly when we are frustrated that he fails to think ahead, understand a complicated rule, anticipate consequences or imagine how we or how anyone else will react. Boys of this age are still very self-oriented: they understand others through assuming others will feel and act as they do, yet their self-understanding is still very underdeveloped.

Parents

* where boys are criticised for falling short, they can easily feel guilty for letting you down and assume there is something wrong with them

* he has to be very grown up and organised at school, so he may want to revert after a trying day and be less responsible at home. Affirmative praise shows empathy and understanding

* find as many ways as possible to spend and enjoy time with him

* whatever he believes you think of him tends to be how he views himself. If he knows you enjoy him, find him fun, reliable and capable, he will work and make friends more confidently when these become important

Teachers

* boys can find it harder to fit in and participate in class activities if home life is stressful. Give any temporary 'loner' a special buddy or use paired activities for a while rather than larger group ones

* be tolerant of young boys' tendency to fidget; they do find it far harder to sit still

* if you feel unsure about the key changes that accompany developmental stages for younger boys and girls, consider taking a course or finding a suitable textbook – it's fascinating!

26 Help him to see who he is

Early childhood is when a boy begins to fill out his idea of who he is and what makes him unique. By the time he reaches seven or eight years old, he will have developed a much clearer sense of what it is he is good at, what his main likes and dislikes are, what and how he prefers to play, how his parents and other adults find him and whether he generally gives pleasure or provokes anger or frustration.

Parents can help a boy to clarify and deepen his identity and ensure it is positive. Instead of simply saying 'I think you're lovely!' we can be far more specific and say 'You are really lovely because you are fun to be with, you are very kind to your friends and share things, you love to paint – even though you hate the clearing up after, you clearly prefer to learn by trying things out rather than just accepting what you're told'. The more detail we can give, while remaining as non-judgemental as possible, the better he will understand and appreciate himself.

Parents

• make him feel he belongs to a clear family grouping and to you. Arrange family outings and events, tell him about his life as a baby and about what your life was like as a child, and involve him in as many of your commitments as is practical or sensible

• experiment with the concept of a 'personality palette'. The more patches of colour that represent different aspects of his personality, skills and preferences you can help to create, describe and place on his personal palette, the more attractive, colourful and detailed will be the picture he can paint of himself

Teachers

• make sure each child is aware of something – his special passion or a particular skill. Feeling positive and proud of that will help him to have a clear and positive sense of who he is and his capabilities

• help him to be aware of his personal preferences that will include how he prefers to work and his favoured activities and subjects. Cover, too, the football team he supports, if any, his favourite food, animal and so on

27 Encourage your pre-teen's developing skills

The pre-teens are renowned as the five years (from eight to twelve) during which children's confidence typically flourishes, provided peer or academic pressures do not grind them down. Their stronger bodies and more capable minds enable boys to view things more reflectively, to be more determined to master complex physical and mental tasks and to work out how to correct mistakes when they get things wrong.

For boys especially, it is their stronger bodies and improved physical coordination that give them their greatest sense of pride. They can climb trees better, kick and hit balls better and begin to perform all manner of stunts with boards and other contraptions. Their skill levels advance by leaps and bounds and they can become quite assertive and competitive to keep their edge of superiority over classmates and friends, as well as try to lord it over their older or younger sisters.

Feeling more confident about who they are, it is their competence and developing sense of judgement that pre-teen boys love to have confirmed and affirmed by adults.

Parents

- admire his growing competence so he feels proud and capable

- give him chances to demonstrate and develop his newly-acquired skills. Ask him to help you with practical tasks, then appreciate his contribution

- watch him doing something he enjoys, even if it is a computer game you think will be tedious

- let him be outside and active as much as possible, provided you have gone through the safety drills

Teachers

- skills that can be applauded and encouraged could include artistic, humour, dramatic, academic, social, communication, sporting, manual dexterity, personal organisation, imagination, physical coordination, musical, memory, listening, sound judgement and empathic skills

28 Accept your pre-teen son's need to act male

My eight-year-old son suddenly developed a whole range of annoying habits, from sniffing outwards (without using a tissue), grunting annoyingly, changing his manner of speaking to generally being stroppy and rude. I felt I was constantly 'on his case'. Then someone explained he was almost certainly copying the latest playground style, identifying more with his mates than the family and needing to experiment with being a 'lad'. Of course she was right.

Gender awareness flourishes in the years between eight and twelve years of age. Boys loosen their emotional ties with their mothers and focus on becoming men. This is the time boys explore, often clumsily, what it means to be male, slanting their thinking and behaviour in ways they consider typical. Tough playground talk often gets brought home.

Pre-teen boys typically play in large groups to feel more powerful. They can become more assertive with female teachers and their mums. They love to master things that previously frightened them, so they take more risks and get up to plenty of mischief.

Parents

*   try not to criticise his new macho 'outfit' continuously. He is a novice trying it on for size – and it won't fit!

*   teach him what is appropriate; say this behaviour or talk is for school, not home

*   as he is trying to separate, maternal praise may be discounted or rejected if it is too gushing. Direct it instead to his achievements and growing competence

*   by understanding why he needs to challenge, you show you approve of and accept him

*   provided he's not endangered, don't 'dis' his friends or any close male role model who is helping him into manhood

Teachers

*   comment favourably on boys' caring, sharing and thoughtful qualities, to indicate these human qualities remain important

*   appreciate pre-teen boys for who they are: their over-confidence often masks a fear of failure

29 Teenage boys like it measured and moderate

Q: *Do you grow out of wanting to be praised?*
A: *You can't not like it. (15)*

Teenage boys still want to hear praise but they want it measured and moderate, not exaggerated or effusive. They are very discriminating by now, and they want it real. They certainly don't want to be flavour of the week one day and in the doghouse the next. Boys are becoming far too independent to be swayed by parental reactions, especially when these seem ill-informed, in either direction. What they appreciate most is being noticed and treated as a source of authority about their welfare, future and progress. They need to be trusted before they can fully trust their individual ability to evaluate accurately and thence do well.

Teenage boys value praise and appreciation more when it is sparing. From parents or teachers alike, they report that when it is in plentiful supply, its value decreases. At this stage, boys like parents just to be around to provide some ballast and chat to, often inconsequentially, when the moment seems right.

Parents

* ask him always how he rates the work, result or performance before you expound. 'That seems a good outcome / result, but it's how *you* judge and see it that matters more'

* ask him if the news is worth passing on. 'Do you want to contact your Dad, or is it not such a big deal?'

* keep it simple: 'Well done', 'That's terrific. Were you pleased?'

* say something at the end of the week rather than every day

* appreciate his views and values more than his daily results so you seem truly interested in and impressed by him rather than obsessed with what he can do

Teachers

* boys enjoy teachers' commendations more readily if these are directed at his hard work and progress rather than at him personally

* ensure that any favourable comments are well supported with detail so he knows exactly what it is he has done well and he can believe it

* for praise to be truly empowering, it must suggest that he has mastered the process just as much as the specific task at hand. 'You have written a very good essay. You are planning your arguments much better, your conclusions are more complete and you are now assessing different approaches. Great'

30 Help teenage boys to have faith in their future

Gregory was an A-grade student. He did well at secondary school and went on to do well at college. He thrived on the regular challenges of coursework and essays and loved the frequent feedback he got from the largely favourable marks. When he started in his first job, he seemed to doubt his performance and flounder. He was so used regular feedback that it took a few months to trust his own judgement and feel at ease.

Self-esteem questionnaires given to boys show that their self-esteem is at its highest at the age of fourteen but then falls gradually to its lowest point at the age of nineteen – the very end of their teens when they come face to face with their future. Life then becomes deadly serious; it is the moment for big decisions – about college, careers and commitment, and the buck has stopped right there in front of them.

Facing such challenge and uncertainty, parents can offer support by commenting favourably on their son's growing maturity and more general competence rather than continuing to highlight exam results.

Parents

- understand and acknowledge the drop in confidence he may face

- make him feel he can make it. 'If you want to . . . it's out there for you to do. You're clearly capable of getting wherever you decide to go. The future is yours and whatever path you choose, we'll back you'

- show respect for his ideas, plans, views and values and assume that others will respect him too. Ultimately, these will be more powerful survival tools than his final results, so reduce the heat on these

Teachers

- encourage teenage boys to look and plan ahead and commend their positive plans

- invite recent pupils to return to describe their personal journeys

- mentors can help enormously to boost individuals' confidence and focus on the possibility of a brighter future than might otherwise be assumed

CHAPTER 5

What to Notice and Encourage: Being creative

It is good practice to find at least three things to notice and comment on positively every day and we should use that comment to point to the past, the present and the future. You should not be asking *if* a child is good at anything, but 'what is my child good at?' because it is undoubtedly true there will be something about what he says or does to notice and appreciate. We just have to be thoughtful and creative.

It is often said that it takes four 'praises' to undo the negative impact of one criticism, so how often we should, or need, to say something encouraging and endorsing depends in part on how critical we have been. Clearly there needs to be a limit: if we say five hurtful or undermining things in one day, then trying to say twenty positive statements that same day to even those out becomes logistically difficult (because we don't necessarily spend that much time together), very confusing for him (because we seem to be blowing hot and cold) and could create an atmosphere that is far too intrusive and contrived (because we have to watch so carefully to spot when to pop in the praise). Young boys' attention is prone to wander freely, so they benefit from plentiful positive feedback delivered frequently and in different ways to keep them on track, as discussed in the next chapter. The older boys become, the less they need or want wall-to-wall praise. Encouragement will become more necessarily context-bound, focused on a time of particular challenge. Provided we don't lay it on thick, boys will come to value these less frequent endorsements and appreciations of their efforts more highly. Don't forget, though, to continue saying how much you enjoy his company and love who he is. The world ahead of him can seem challenging, even frightening, and he will need every ounce of confidence he can muster.

There is a vast range of possible attributes and achievements to notice. If we focus on a single area, for example school marks and work, we have to ask about these every day in order to know what to say. And whichever aspect of his life we comment on could become the part of him he feels we value most, and the one he's most likely to choose to sabotage if he ever feels the need to get his own back.

If we pride ourselves on offering a tolerant, warm and accepting home, we should aim to value, notice and openly appreciate: all aspects of his personality – fears and foibles as well as robustness; skills and talents; general capability; attitudes towards others and the ability to deal with problems.

31 Appreciate his thinking skills

Boys are, essentially, doers; they are action men. They like to be noisy, active, on the go almost all of the time. This energy is a joy to see and is impressive. It may be exhausting to have to deal with but most of us would give anything to regain that early vigour – the power to keep going and not stop until we drop, apparently effortlessly. However, they have to learn to think and reflect. Many boys seem to find reflection unnatural. We can help by ensuring they have quiet thinking time, by commenting positively when they show they have thought something through and by encouraging the habit of asking two or three more probing questions before they claim they have understood enough.

Boys in fact think all the time; when they decide what game to play or what clothes to put on in the morning (though sometimes we grimace when they select the item closest to hand as a quick solution!); when they work out how to mend a broken toy, solve an argument with a friend or suggest a suitable present for a brother or sister. He is forced to reflect when we ask him to explain his behaviour. Reflection is a useful and protective tool because it will help him to think ahead, get on with others and stay clear of trouble.

Parents

• chat about recent hours or days and recall what has happened that he might have found fun, scary or difficult. 'It's interesting you've mentioned that. Why did you find it scary?'

• invite him to plan and think ahead when there's free time to fill or there's an unfamiliar situation to face

• appreciate his choices: 'That's a good idea of what to play!', 'I like how you put that jumper and those trousers together'

Teachers

• who's a good problem-solver here?

• I very much liked your ideas about what Ben was really thinking in that story

• ask him how he would have liked a story or game to end

32 Encourage his sociable side

Girls are natural talkers; boys are less so. Boys tend to talk later, read later, have a smaller vocabulary as a result and spend less time in intimate conversation with their friends, a pattern that remains during adolescence and adds further to the verbal gender gap. On top of this, boys' fine motor skills also develop later so they can find writing a slow and often messy business. Words, whether spoken or written, are so often not boys' strong point.

Being more tongue-tied and less adroit at expressing themselves, they are often more prone to embarrassment and shyness and would prefer to avoid social gatherings. It is typical for a boy to appear momentarily at a family event then strangely evaporate, or to round up other soul mates and depart to computers and dens!

However, social skills are valuable and emotional literacy requires a good vocabulary to describe feelings as well as understand behaviour. It is important to reward boys when they join in, welcome their friends, discourage isolation and encourage conversation.

Parents

- value a range of skills that will help him in social situations, such as helpfulness, understanding, kindness and thoughtfulness, willingness to share and sorting out or stepping away from arguments

- expect that he joins you sometimes when you visit friends or relatives

- try to have at the very least one family meal each week to encourage conversation and friendly banter

Teachers

- boys often prefer to work alone rather than in a group, because they don't have to share or explain, can be competitive and can do it their way without having to compromise. But group-based tasks encourage sensitivity and sociability. Both ways of working should be included in structured learning

- groups of both mixed and same gender help boys and girls to appreciate each other's strengths and learn from each other

33 Acknowledge that he tried hard

Did you try hard and do your best? That's what matters.

Acknowledging effort is not a soft option, for progress is made at every stage on the learning journey. Getting there is at least as important as arriving; and each arrival point becomes a past staging post from which the learner moves on. It can represent a bigger step forward for someone to realise finally what he's been doing wrong and work out for himself how to correct it than to get something right at the first attempt but with little awareness of why it was correct.

Effort is important. No one achieves anything significant without it. Effort is something accomplished involving concentration; it means you give it your all. Young children find it hard to concentrate and they will probably have a poor appreciation of what 'trying hard' actually means. But if a young boy's more limited efforts are not respected and valued, it may be harder for him to make the necessary effort when he's older, has more control over it and when the results might matter more.

Parents

* ask him what he means when he says, 'But I tried really hard' before you condemn it as a weak excuse

* ask for specifics such as: time spent on it, amount of any diversion such as TV, computer or phone calls, whether he took the time to look something up if he wasn't sure or whether he took time to check it over

* if you have every reason to trust him and he said he did his best, not knowing how to do it differently, let it rest at that

Teachers

* do you encourage your students to understand what the terms 'effort' and 'trying' mean?

* do you talk about how difficult it can be to persevere, and what students think and feel when they get despondent? Ask anyone who finds a way through when discouraged to describe what he or she does to achieve this

34 Notice his organisational skills

Teachers say that boys are noticeably less organised and independent than girls when they start secondary school, which interferes with their work. They leave books at home, sports bags on buses or forget the deadline for homework. It is a handicap. But the response of most parents or significant others is to take over and do more things for the boy in their care to avoid disasters. This might make us feel better: we avoid feeling embarrassed when the school complains and we can see our involvement as a gesture of caring when they become harder to hug; but it is not helpful. Boys need to face the consequences of their disorganisation for only then will they make genuine efforts to change their ways.

But we do not have to wait until things get really bad. There are other options. Well before rock bottom, we can notice plenty of small examples of organisation and self-management and comment favourably on these. Tidying just a corner of a bedroom is progress; returning for an item remembered at the last minute is better than forgetting it when they are out of range; and prioritising commitments on a busy Saturday shows forward thinking.

Parents

* suggest strategies to aid his self-organisation, such as making lists, writing reminders on sticky notes or having a daily kit or 'to do' list

* ask him how he prefers to remember things. It must become his project, not yours or it may not work

* notice when he manages to think and prepare ahead. If it is his way to get everything together at the last minute and it works, that's good enough

* better to applaud the developing skills than exude frustration or sneer at how far he still has to go. He may be organised in some spheres, just not in the ones you'd like!

Teachers

* his work may look messy in presentation but if it demonstrates an organised approach this should be highlighted and commended

* a focus on meta-learning – learning how to learn – will automatically encourage boys to consider their procedures and preparation

35 Value his imagination, however fanciful!

I'm a knight. This ruler is my sword and I'm going to slay the dragon! This little figure is Gandrill – he's lord of the fire and in charge of all these dwarves who need his fire to make their special daggers that have the power to turn the evil goblins to dust!

A boy's imagination represents him. It is his own personal creation and not only gives him a sense of freedom but also some productive control over his time. Fantasy allows endless possibilities: he can explore the rare experience of feeling powerful because he can create stories in which he takes a lead role and he has unlimited strength. Being in charge of the story, nothing can go wrong for him unless he so wills it, so he can feel totally safe. If we join in on his terms and accept the role he wants us to play, he in effect is in charge of us too, which will help him to accept our bidding much of the rest of the time.

Fantasy encourages mental flexibility and creativity and both help later with schoolwork. It is very important that we appreciate and value his ability to draw, play and explore imaginatively and that we occasionally play along with it, entering his fantasy.

Parents

* don't devalue any imaginative play. It is part of him, gives him great skills and increases his self-knowledge and confidence

* older boys explore imagination through fantasy. It is not babyish but a healthy counter to the daily grind, provided he can leave it behind when appropriate

* if you join in an imaginative game, don't suddenly talk about the shopping you need to do or what he'd like for tea as it will shatter his creation and his belief that you take him seriously

Teachers

* fanciful imagination can become distracting, but boys need to be able to be themselves and be encouraged to take risks with possibilities

* boys' imagination sometimes appears in the form of humour or silly pranks. They clown about both to get attention and status but also to exercise their minds and find new ways to play with ideas

36 Enjoy his humour

Humour adds joy to life. Around the age of seven or eight something very important happens to the way children's minds work. They can look at themselves from the outside, think in abstract categories far more easily and can play with ideas and see new links. Any parent of a child of this age will tell you that it is at this time they constantly get asked to laugh at what are usually, to begin with, very bad jokes that their children consider utterly hilarious. Children's joke books tend to be pitched at this age group. They can recount some, often picked up from the playground, which they cannot possibly under-stand but they find an alternative explanation that makes sense to them. But it's not just the jokes themselves they enjoy; they take great delight in entering that hitherto closed adult world of telling jokes and being in the powerful position of making other people laugh. They become, in effect, the family's very own court jester.

Once we laugh, out of either politeness or genuine mirth, he won't stop. The show goes on, and on, and on. It gives him huge pleasure and great pride to entertain in this way. We must play the appre-ciative audience and allow him to exercise his new mental muscles and have fun playing with ideas and words.

Parents

* be patient, and try to laugh – or groan – when you are told a joke even if you have heard it plenty of times before

* magic tricks are visual jokes that play with the viewer's perceptions and expectations. Encourage any interest in magic, and be tolerant of the performance that he may want to arrange for the family

Teachers

* around the age of ten, boys begin to understand the real humour of jokes and enjoy telling them and making them up. Boys' humour should be valued and given a place in the classroom – though they need to learn when is a good or bad time!

* linked to this, around the same age boys can become the class clown, in part because they gain status when they make others laugh, and in part to avoid answering questions. It might help to defuse an irritating situation to invite the main 'culprit' to prepare a real entertainment session

37 Welcome creativity – and the risks and mess involved

Every human being has the capacity to be creative. Young children find it easiest, because they have less idea of what is expected or what is right and wrong. For them, experimentation is fun and helps them to feel in charge and powerful – free from rules and other restrictions. Young boys will not yet have absorbed gender-related social conventions about what boys generally do, so they can all be encouraged to try out a wide range of fun activities, including cooking or painting.

Older boys express their creativity in less organised ways. We should not devalue any activity simply because it seems to lack purpose. Whittling sticks with a penknife, building outdoor camps, mucking about with mud or making up rules for a variety of games are all creative pursuits.

Creativity is the expression of originality: it helps children to discover their identity and experience directly the ways in which they are unique.

Parents

* it is not just girls who like to paint. Offer him plenty of opportunities to carry on drawing, colouring, painting and modelling beyond nursery school

* the majority of celebrity chefs are men, so don't think it wrong to encourage boys to cook and make up recipes

* collage-style pictures can be created from discarded rubbish, fabric oddments or from twigs, leaves, petals and plant seeds

Teachers

* boys can become more easily and deeply absorbed in a creative activity if they keep quiet. Try to limit the chat as they explore their ideas and discover what they can create

* clearing up afterwards helps to instil good organisational habits and encourages a sensible allocation of time. Invite students to gauge how much time is needed

45 Hugs are for sharing

A hug is a physical gesture that enables us to share any feelings of joy or disappointment. It is essentially non-judgemental because it is empathic and it says, 'I'm happy for you' as well as 'I am sad or happy or pleased with you', in both senses of the phrase. It is a two-way gesture, for the hug has to be accepted and reciprocated. When it finishes, it leaves our son holding the feeling and there is nothing we can take away from him and use for our benefit.

Some families don't feel comfortable with such physical closeness. They don't hug much, or kiss or express themselves. And boys, as they enter their pre-teens or teens, often reject particularly maternal embraces. Passing on a hug, from a pet dog or cat, or from a soft toy that's an old favourite may be one way to make the gesture of embrace without forcing one on him.

Parents

- boys typically develop passions that span particular sports, kinds of music, knowledge about space and astronomy, cars, military hardware or for books based on particular characters. Show interest and help him to find out more to endorse his choices and values

- if he develops a passion for animals, it means he cares for creatures that need to be looked after. We should respect this tenderness

Teachers

- try to find out about individual students' passions and values and make reference to these respectfully

46 Say it with surprises!

Surprises are another way of saying thank you, or showing appreciation or love. A favourite meal, a plate of pieces of fruit arranged as a funny face, space ship or rocket, a surprise outing, a balloon that you have written or drawn on, an unexpected small present, are all examples of surprises that can show appreciation of some special effort or simply to say how much you have enjoyed him that week or weekend.

Friday treats are a lovely way to sign off a school week. If any boy wants to know what the treat is 'for', we can reply: to mark the end of a week's work or 'because you are you!'

Parents

- treats and surprises don't have to be earned or deserved

- if reward is the message, treats could raise the question, 'What if I'm not good next time?' and so could become tainted

- the pleasure is the surprise and the thought, not the object itself. It can be really simple – and cheap!

- 'today, just for fun, we're going on a mystery night walk with torches!'

Teachers

- curriculum pressures leave little space for surprises but the end of term is a good moment to appreciate everyone's commitment and have fun

40 Go deeper – accept his fears and feelings

My biggest problem is my Dad who keeps saying, 'Be a man' every time I cry. I know I'm a boy but it's so hard to hold it in. I worry I'll be a giant failure. (12)

'When a child cannot be sad or lonely or angry because his parents will not be pleased with him if he is, he will feel he cannot be the person he knows himself to be and he will believe that he is unsatisfactory.' (Dorothy Rowe, author and psychotherapist.) A child whose fears and feelings are ignored or denied will not only feel misunderstood but also very alone. Apart from our psychological inheritance, it is our feelings that make us who we are and give us our sense of self. We experience these, often intensely, before we have the vocabulary to describe them and they are our first building blocks. That certain things interest us, upset, frustrate or hurt us, give us pleasure or make us defensive and react selfishly creates our individuality. If we can recognise all his particular moods and characteristics we will demonstrate a deep understanding of him and how he sees his world.

By accepting his dilemmas at his level, he will be free to be and grow; nothing less.

Parents

* our feelings are the building blocks of our selves

* allow him to feel disappointed or angry if he doesn't do well – or if anything that you say doesn't go down well

* if you take the time and trouble to understand the feelings that may explain his behaviour, you will find out more about him

* it is normal for boys to feel angry, insulted, hostile and proud, for boys are, like us, whole human beings. Ask yourself why his reactions bother you; don't put the pressure on him to deny or ignore them

Teachers

* acknowledge boys' feelings, though ensure that the rules about acceptable ways for them to be expressed are maintained

CHAPTER 6

The Language of Praise: Ways to say it, and do it

Human beings communicate in many subtle and less subtle ways. We use words, touch, facial expressions and a range of different physical and symbolic gestures. We often merely sense the pleasure we have given someone through the tone of voice they use or the way they look at us. We often interpret a number of reactions and piece together an overall impression. As adults, we don't always need to have it spelt out every time that someone considers we have done well.

If praise is valuable and worthwhile because it helps boys to feel acknowledged, noticed, approved of, valued, accepted and appreciated as well as helping them to be successful, it follows that there are many ways to bring this about: praise does not always have to be given in words. Boys too, as they mature, can appreciate the more subtle signs and know we are grateful. Although language is what we tend to use to express our delight, pleasure and surprise when a child has done well, by extending our praise repertoire we will limit the dangers, already noted, associated with spoken praise, and sometimes surprise them, which is always fun!

If children thrive when they are sure we enjoy them, having fun together when they do well is important. We should not make fun of praise or make fun of them by using and twisting or sending up praise, but the whole family can have plenty of fun discovering different ways to express love and appreciation and finding approaches that are lighter in tone.

49 Let siblings in on it

It should be part of family living that siblings value and appreciate each other's particular achievements. Praise shouldn't always be issued from the top down. But this won't happen without everyone first having heard you say 'well done' or 'that's a lovely . . .', simple phrases that are easy for all children to use. Of course, no child should have to take over a parent's responsibility for affirming or accepting a brother or sister; nevertheless, where there is a genuine sharing of family appreciation, and celebration and praise is not treated as a treasured winner's cup or instrument of advantage that is exploited, each child will feel more generous and open with praise and less threatened by or possessive of it.

Difficulties can arise where one sibling has talents or interests that enable him to be more enthusiastic and all-round successful than another. He may then attract more admiration from friends and family, creating an imbalance between siblings. If this happens, ask the surrounding admirers to cool off and make sure the other siblings receive plenty of loving attention and appreciation – often more nourishing than accolade. Be careful, too, not to blur the line between the achievement and the child.

Parents

* vary the words, style and response to avoid sounding like a stuck record. Children very quickly switch off and imagine the rest once they hear the intro, especially when we nag. Even repetitive praise gets to sound stale

* try such responses as: 'That's lovely!', 'Brilliant!', 'Well done!', 'That's great!', 'Thanks for doing that', 'That was sensible', 'How thoughtful!', 'What a great idea!'

* if he begins to look at you askance instead of beaming with pride, go easy because you are probably overdoing it; save your comments for something that matters more to him

Teachers

* comments on written work need to be full and explicit but spoken approval can be short. 'I really liked that story / your arguments / the line you took. Take a look at my comments'

* warmer tones of voice and full-hearted attention convey approval too

50 Watch out for 'I' phrases

Praise should focus more on the event or the child than on us. Once we start sentences with 'I . . .' the emphasis becomes our view of things. 'I like the way . . .' 'I'm very pleased', 'I think you could have done more to . . .' 'I was so surprised you did so well . . .', 'I am convinced everything will go well for you because you have prepared so thoroughly.' The earlier discussion of the purpose of praise highlighted such things as acknowledgement, attention and affirmation. Children love to please their parents when they are young, but as they get older they need less of their parents' pleasure and more affirmation and confirmation that they have judged things well and are on the right track, which will encourage confidence.

If a boy is hungry for praise he will find any format rewarding, including all 'I . . .' phrases, but these won't help to wean him off any unhealthy reliance on our judgement. If he starts to sense he is being manipulated or too closely monitored, he may simply ignore them all. On the other hand, phrases such as 'You did really well', 'That was a brilliant result' or 'The way you were able to reflect on that test and spot where you went wrong was impressive', are more focused on the process and are statements of fact that centre on him, not of judgement that centre on you.

Parents

* 'you are lovely as you are, *and* you're extra special to me!' is less loaded than 'I love you as you are' – especially if he has just done something to please you

* 'you handled that really well. Others might have lost their cool. Well done!' is preferable to, 'I really liked the way you handled that'

* 'you're such fun to be around' is less of a burden to carry than 'I love being around you when you're this cheerful'

* free him: focus your remarks on his ability to set about tasks well rather than offering your opinion on the outcome

Teachers

* 'you've clearly got the measure of this problem now. This was a terrific assignment and shows what you are really capable of' is more convincing than, 'I am pleased you have understood this problem and done this piece of work so well'

43 Talk with touch

Touch has its own language. It can say so much in such a variety of ways and it need only be fleeting. Touch, for example, is an intimate way to demonstrate an equality of regard and respect. It can express feelings more quickly than words and although it is less precise, it has the great advantage of allowing the receiver to read what he wants – and needs to hear – into it. It is therefore more likely to 'hit home' and satisfy. Touch is certainly less open to misinterpretation than streams of worthy words and is an important gesture of approval, appreciation and giving. Its capacity to convey understanding makes it also serve as a useful way to demonstrate empathy.

A child who lives around adults that never touch him, even if they say the 'right' praise words, will feel ignored, unworthy of attention, inferior, misunderstood and, eventually, ashamed – the very opposite of what we hope praise will achieve.

knows it. These can all have counterproductive consequences that are explored in this chapter.

The dangers that are associated with the wrong kind of attention, be it indiscriminate praise or constant criticism, include perfectionism (explored in Chapter Ten), stress-inducing pressure, burn-out and opting out and, perhaps curiously, feelings of low self-worth. We might intend that our son feel pride and satisfaction, but this is not guaranteed. These outcomes, admittedly, lie at the extreme end; signs of interim difficulty or more serious trouble ahead can include secretiveness, mild cheating and copying of other people's work and learned helplessness.

The characteristic common to all the mistakes reviewed here is placing our concerns and desires before our son's feelings and wishes: a failure to treat him as an autonomous human being. Each child should, then, be allowed to be who he is and not be compared to anyone else or used by us as a vehicle to make good any missed opportunities of our own that we may now regret. He should be put in charge of his growth as much as possible, given the freedom to say no or stop and be offered every opportunity to do well for his own pleasure, not simply to please us. Parents often need to step in and help a child over a sticky patch, for example not understanding some maths or getting disenchanted with their progress on a musical instrument and wanting to give up; but when he has overcome the problem we should withdraw, allowing him from then on to set his own pace and direction.

44 Use fun gestures

My teenage son did very well in some important exams. I wanted to show my appreciation and acknowledge his achievement without using money, gifts or getting too heavy about it because he'd worked hard for his own satisfaction, not to please me. I bought a large sheet of stiff card, selected a handful of photos from the family collection representing different stages of his life and stuck these on, writing an amusing comment against each one that made reference to his potential. He thought it was silly but funny and he loved the gesture! He still has it, eight years on.

Money is not the only way to measure value or express pleasure, though it can be very easy to sign cheques. Although boys love to get something new that they have longed for, they also appreciate being on the receiving end of an original gesture that takes time and special effort, something tailored to his passions and which makes him laugh. It will almost certainly be remembered for longer; and birthdays can be utilised to realise the wish list.

Parents

* other fun gestures that can show our appreciation could include:
  - arranging a special outing as a treat
  - preparing his favourite meal
  - having his friend over to sleep overnight
  - buying a new cushion, lamp or bedcover for his room

Teachers

* boys love quizzes, which work well as an end of term treat to recognise the collective class progress. Simple prizes of sweets, chocolate or party bag gifts make it even more fun and special

38 Go deep – endorse his values and beliefs

If one purpose of praise is to make a boy feel good about who he is inside rather than rely on a range of external shows of such things as clothes, toys, kit or talents to make him feel comfortable with himself, we need to respect his values and beliefs.

Younger boys will not have developed any consistent system of values for us to appreciate but they do attach great importance to their friendships and their play. They also possess a natural, passionate concern for fairness that we ignore at our peril. Their beliefs are manifest in the sense they make of their immediate world: these form the structure that creates coherence when they face and have to manage confusing events.

From ten or so onwards, their ability to think in more abstract and conceptual ways and see things from other people's standpoint encourages many boys latch onto passions and concerns that focus on others. Whether it is religion, vegetarianism, ecology, astronomy or alternative music, we should endorse their right to develop their own values and interests and respect their beliefs.

Parents

* 'here's a hug [and make the gesture]. When you're ready for it, come and get it!'

* 'is your happiness for sharing? How about me giving you a hug, then?'

* 'that's made me really happy. Give me a hug so I can share it with you'

Teachers

* teachers cannot hug children, but they are able to stand close or pat an arm or shoulder instead or express their delight in words

39 Appreciate his practical skills and competence

Growing children feel such pride each time they conquer something they were not capable of achieving previously. They spend so many years dependent in some way or other it gives them a sense of freedom and autonomy when they grow tall enough, strong enough, dextrous enough and responsible enough to manage themselves or undertake tasks that combine skill and knowledge that can help others.

Boys tend to have strong spatial skills; they can see how things fit together, can arrange or view objects in different places in their minds and hold information such as routes, maps and wiring layouts in a clear manner that makes them easy to remember. This makes many of them good at building and mending things and especially adept at solving computing problems.

Practical skills help a boy to manage on his own, valuable not so much for survival but because autonomy is the ultimate expression of self – the way all of us experience and activate ourselves. Competencies, then, help to define and action our sense of self and boost self-esteem.

Parents

• write down all the things your son is good at and likes to do. Think of ways you could put any of these skills to practical use in the home

• if he is too young to be of genuine help, encourage him to come and hold things for you or pass things, and he will learn at the same time

• give him any discarded bit of electrical appliance or other equipment (if safe) when it has broken to take apart and explore

Teachers

• where a student mentions something he has done, made or mended at home, compliment the skill involved. 'Sounds like you're good at that sort of thing, Tom. Want a job at my house!?'

• as boys develop their manual dexterity, show how this can be put to practical use. 'Wow. That would make you good at electronics / tuning my guitar / dicing vegetables / getting my baby daughter dressed in the morning!'

47 Let him feel whatever he feels

My six-year-old son's school report was very complimentary. His teacher was especially positive about how well he was doing academically. When I said 'Well done', he buried his face and choked, 'It's a stupid report. What's the point of saying I'm good when it's so easy?'

Affirmation means we accept him as he is, not fashioned according to what we want to see because that makes life simpler. A boy who does well and thrives (for these are not the same things) is someone who knows himself and feels free to 'be'. If he feels able to feel sad, frustrated, happy, disappointed, angry, hateful, confident, frightened or excited, he will probably experience his parent's tolerance and continuing presence and love throughout all these as a sign he can trust them, and himself, because they accept and trust all of him. He will feel understood, and if given the scope to decide when he pulls out the stops, when he coasts, when he explores his developing interests and how he allocates his time, he will be sufficiently confident to manage this sensibly.

Parents

• accept that his fearful beliefs are real for him. He should not be told boys don't believe that nonsense and should not feel scared of things like monsters, the dark or deep water

• notice his happy moods from his body movements, shining eyes or his bouncy walk, and say, 'You seem very cheerful today. Something nice must have happened. Lucky you!' and let him keep it to himself if he doesn't want to tell you why

• notice his sad moods, too, and accept that he will feel angry, jealous, resentful, lonely or even hate you, and tell him that's natural and okay. Never deny his difficult feelings

Teachers

• some boys are very sensitive and squeamish. Prevent other children in the class from picking on anyone and teasing them for their natural feelings

• learning can be frightening. Accept that some reluctance to try could mask a deep fear of failure, and try to get to the bottom of this. The learning environment must be made safe for boys who lack confidence

• fears and feelings, indeed, all strong emotions, make learning difficult. Understand what a boy might be going through in his personal life, what pattern and expectation of relationships he brings into school, and consider how these may affect him

48 Allow him to say it

It is not necessarily pig-headed or offensively arrogant for a child to believe he has done well and admit so. Indeed, secondary school students are increasingly encouraged to judge the quality of their own work as part of well-organised self-assessment programmes. Many nursery schools, influenced by recent government guidance, invite children as young as three to 'plan, do, then review' the effectiveness of their chosen approaches to various tasks.

The possible downside of openly admitting to having been successful is pride and conceit. Children quickly identify 'stuck up' braggers and can turn against them ruthlessly; indeed, most children possess a deep seated reticence about their talents and are not natural boasters. Perhaps those who do, simply copy parents! But the danger is avoided if we make clear that his particular abilities do not make him better as a person than someone without those talents and that he should never look down on anyone who performs differently. The knowledge that he's done his best and is doing well at whatever activity should stay private to him.

Parents

* teach that 'good at' means 'different from' not 'better than' in anything other than comparative skill terms

* always ask, 'Are you pleased with it?' or 'Would you praise this?' and let him decide and say it

* boys tend to overestimate their work in self-assessment. If he says it's great and he's really happy with it, ask what he might do differently next time to make it even better. He'll then be forced to look at the room for improvement

Teachers

* 'I was very happy with this. Well done. Did you think you'd done it well?'

* encourage self-assessment, backed up with peer review and peer moderation

* before you write the end of term report, ask students to anticipate your remarks. If there is a major discrepancy between your view and a student's, in either direction, discuss it with him later

41 Keep approval simple

The more we spell it out, the more laboured, false, inappropriate or overdone the praise can become. To avoid a child feeling burdened or uncomfortable and even misunderstood by our outpourings we should, quite simply, keep our expressions of approval simple.

Approval, as has been explained, focuses on the individual. It puts the child in the spotlight, which is why he may squirm if it becomes exaggerated. Appreciation, on the other hand, relates to the task and therefore sometimes needs to be more detailed and specific (though still not disproportionate) so our child knows he can trust our appreciation.

Even praise that describes and offers a boy an account of what has pleased us (sometimes called 'descriptive praise') can be kept simple if we say things such as 'Well cycled', 'Well caught', 'Well tidied' or 'Well tried' instead of 'That was clever, how you cycled that tight circle'. Leaving some detail out allows him to decide for himself what it was that was good and makes him less dependent on our assessment and freer to make up his own mind.

Parents

* show joy in each of your children's varied milestones, pleasures and personalities

* younger children can draw a picture as a gesture for a brother. Older ones can say well done, ask about the event and watch the play, match or performance

* don't allow one child in particular to get all your acclaim and attention. If there is potentially destructive jealousy, the balance could be awry

* view a child's talent as 'his chosen thing' rather than as anything remarkable

Teachers

* positively value each child as an individual

* raise the suggestion that a sibling in the same school could be pleased to know about some special outcome

* beware actually telling a brother or sister about their sibling's good efforts, in case it is misinterpreted as an underhanded incentive to improve

42 Say it with a smile

Sometimes children don't need to hear anything spoken. Beaming smiles are enough. When they reach the tape in the school race and turn round to see if we saw their effort or their triumph, a smile and a nod from a distance is all we can give – and it is often more than enough.

Parents

* we can use commercially available peel-off coloured smiley faces, sparingly, as a surprise or reminder of our love especially at times we cannot be there. But make no mistake: these will be no substitute for the real thing!

* for a younger boy, we can draw a simple smiley face on a small white board or blackboard in his bedroom after bedtime for him to find on waking. But beware of forgetting to do so if it has become a nightly routine

Teachers

* smiley faces drawn or stuck on the end of work show you are pleased with the result but they don't offer useful detailed feedback where that is more appropriate

CHAPTER 7

Common Mistakes to Try to Avoid

Despite the best of intentions and our wish to help boys do well and show how much we love and appreciate them, we can still either say the wrong thing entirely or say the right thing at the wrong time or in the wrong way and, through clumsiness or ignorance, put our foot in it.

Though it may surprise some people, the worst offence is not necessarily criticism, some of which may be justified and valuable. It is not helpful to protect our child from every nuance of disapproval or disappointment. When he has misjudged or failed to understand things or ignored clear guidance, he should receive straightforward yet constructive, supportive explanations of what he can do differently next time. Constructive criticism is a far more helpful response than alternatives such as harsh punishment, scathing sarcasm, turning a 'blind eye' or offering fulsome praise for effort even if the outcome was way below expectation – and your son

Parents

* experiment with little touches of appreciation instead of using words

* if touch has disappeared from your relationship with your growing son, sit close to him as he watches TV, ruffle his hair when he comes in from school or play with his hands and fingers as you chat with him at bedtime

* if he finds your approaches difficult, ask him before you do it so you know he feels ready for it

Teachers

* of course it is not usually appropriate for professionals to touch male students, especially as they get older. Nevertheless, if you stand quite close while you look over work, you can show he is acceptable and you feel comfortable in his presence

* consider whether shaking a boy's hand or presenting your outstretched palm as athletes do is an alternative acceptable way to demonstrate approval and appreciation

51 Think about why you're saying it

When we consider whether to give what we may see as the 'gift' of praise, we look first at what our child has done and whether the behaviour or circumstance warrants it. Our focus is therefore on him and is context bound, time-limited and top-down: the conscious part of our attention is fixed on him. But less obvious ulterior motives often lurk behind our apparently altruistic actions or comments that have more to do with us – our dreams, desires and fears – than with him. We applaud certain attributes to help him achieve aims we consider desirable. We can so easily try to turn him into what we want him to be.

At one level, this is inevitable. Of course it is a parent's job to encourage socially acceptable behaviour and discourage actions that will get him into trouble. We do shape children's behaviour and should do so, as gardeners prune growing plants so they develop stronger stems and larger flowers. But we should be careful not to take a cutting from ourselves and graft it onto them or cut and style so much that they need walls or wires to hold them up. We should not contrive to bolster our own vulnerable self-worth with a child's success or fail to give him the autonomy he needs.

Parents

- consider if you are making a point of being positive to compensate for being very preoccupied recently. Could you be saying 'the right things' to make him feel more loving towards you because you need more support?

- if the answer to either of these is 'yes' or 'possibly', beware your motives and manipulation. Better to address the issue directly or at source!

- watch carefully how he responds to the different ways in which you express approval and delight

- as much as you can, put it back to him: 'Yes, I do like it, but the more important thing is whether you do.' 'To me, you did very well, but were you pleased with the result?'

Teachers

- if praise is natural, it will roll off the tongue without much forethought

- individual boys who have a despondent personality may need more encouragement than others

45 Hugs are for sharing

A hug is a physical gesture that enables us to share any feelings of joy or disappointment. It is essentially non-judgemental because it is empathic and it says, 'I'm happy for you' as well as 'I am sad or happy or pleased with you', in both senses of the phrase. It is a two-way gesture, for the hug has to be accepted and reciprocated. When it finishes, it leaves our son holding the feeling and there is nothing we can take away from him and use for our benefit.

Some families don't feel comfortable with such physical closeness. They don't hug much, or kiss or express themselves. And boys, as they enter their pre-teens or teens, often reject particularly maternal embraces. Passing on a hug, from a pet dog or cat, or from a soft toy that's an old favourite may be one way to make the gesture of embrace without forcing one on him.

Parents

* instead of 'good' we can say clever, organised, thoughtful, helpful or creative; or just say 'You're a happy boy'. If he has done something he's pleased with, that's how he'll be feeling

* instead of labelling him 'bad' or 'naughty' we should turn it around to our view: 'I found that rather selfish', 'I didn't like that behaviour'

* if we want to convey in simple terms our delight in his existence, we can say, 'Mmm. You're my lovely boy!' which suggests he's lovable, the pre-requisite for self-esteem

* boys who do most of what you ask but hold a bit of themselves back are good enough!

Teachers

* 'very good' on a piece of work tells the student very little about what he did right and he may not be sure of this. Instead you could write, 'Very well argued', 'Very well researched', 'Very good use of detail', 'Lovely descriptions – I saw it all!'

* 'good' boys should be not so good to teach; good students should always question and challenge

46 Say it with surprises!

Surprises are another way of saying thank you, or showing appreciation or love. A favourite meal, a plate of pieces of fruit arranged as a funny face, space ship or rocket, a surprise outing, a balloon that you have written or drawn on, an unexpected small present, are all examples of surprises that can show appreciation of some special effort or simply to say how much you have enjoyed him that week or weekend.

Friday treats are a lovely way to sign off a school week. If any boy wants to know what the treat is 'for', we can reply: to mark the end of a week's work or 'because you are you!'

Parents

- treats and surprises don't have to be earned or deserved

- if reward is the message, treats could raise the question, 'What if I'm not good next time?' and so could become tainted

- the pleasure is the surprise and the thought, not the object itself. It can be really simple – and cheap!

- 'today, just for fun, we're going on a mystery night walk with torches!'

Teachers

- curriculum pressures leave little space for surprises but the end of term is a good moment to appreciate everyone's commitment and have fun

54 Don't take the credit for his success

Sometimes parents invest so much of their time and effort in helping their son to achieve the hoped-for success that they are convinced it could never have been achieved without them. They may have spent hours coaching him or sacrificed a great deal to pay for specialist tuition; they may have imposed strict practice regimes or been genuinely supportive when something went awry, that their child was able to find his own way back to confidence through tolerance. This enables them to take responsibility for the success, expressed either privately or openly, which can then underrate their son's contribution. Offering rewards and incentives can have the same effect, making parental intervention the critical factor. When parents steal some of the credit, which is what this amounts to, a child may feel empty and used simply as a tool to generate a parent's self-esteem.

Comments such as 'I told you that you were a "natural", that's why I signed you up for the course' or 'Congratulations for getting into the team. Aren't you pleased now that I put you on that healthier diet?' clearly claim some of the credit.

Parents

* our feelings are the building blocks of our selves

* allow him to feel disappointed or angry if he doesn't do well – or if anything that you say doesn't go down well

* if you take the time and trouble to understand the feelings that may explain his behaviour, you will find out more about him

* it is normal for boys to feel angry, insulted, hostile and proud, for boys are, like us, whole human beings. Ask yourself why his reactions bother you; don't put the pressure on him to deny or ignore them

Teachers

* acknowledge boys' feelings, though ensure that the rules about acceptable ways for them to be expressed are maintained

55 'I'm so proud of you!'

Which of the following would you be most likely to say? 'I'm really proud of you for managing that!'; 'I hope you feel proud of yourself for doing that – you deserved to do well after all that effort'; 'You probably feel really proud to have achieved that'; 'I feel so proud of you and proud to have you as my child.'

When I talked to a group of fifteen-year-old boys at an academic secondary school, they all agreed that the parental phrase they most love to hate was, 'I'm so proud of you'. They found it hard to explain why this response grated so much; but the problem seemed to relate to it being 'over the top' as well as causing discomfort with having a parent too emotionally involved in their work. They did not want the responsibility for delivering or maintaining their parent's sense of pride and they certainly had not worked hard for a particular test or exam in order that their parent could feel that way – they had done it for themselves and for their own reasons.

Our role should be to enable our son to feel proud of himself, independently and regardless of our feelings because he knows what he set out to achieve and the effort that he needed to apply.

Parents

* keep comments as free from judgement as possible. 'You probably felt really proud when you heard that' implies that if he did feel that, you can understand why. If not, no matter

* even 'I hope you feel proud of that result' implies that if he doesn't, he should because your view counts

* pride can be an overweening opinion: be careful you're not exaggerating his achievement

* if you attach too much virtue to one attribute and he'd prefer not to carry the weight of your hope, pride might, indeed, come before a fall if he decides to stop trying

Teachers

* you can be proud of the achievement of a class – proud of everyone or of your professional input; but your pride is less relevant to any individual's success

* 'I am really impressed with your progress', 'You deserve to feel proud of your achievement' or 'I'm so pleased you have understood things and can now work closer to your true ability level' are more appropriate remarks for individual boys

49 Let siblings in on it

It should be part of family living that siblings value and appreciate each other's particular achievements. Praise shouldn't always be issued from the top down. But this won't happen without everyone first having heard you say 'well done' or 'that's a lovely . . .', simple phrases that are easy for all children to use. Of course, no child should have to take over a parent's responsibility for affirming or accepting a brother or sister; nevertheless, where there is a genuine sharing of family appreciation, and celebration and praise is not treated as a treasured winner's cup or instrument of advantage that is exploited, each child will feel more generous and open with praise and less threatened by or possessive of it.

Difficulties can arise where one sibling has talents or interests that enable him to be more enthusiastic and all-round successful than another. He may then attract more admiration from friends and family, creating an imbalance between siblings. If this happens, ask the surrounding admirers to cool off and make sure the other siblings receive plenty of loving attention and appreciation – often more nourishing than accolade. Be careful, too, not to blur the line between the achievement and the child.

Parents

- imagine praise as a biscuit: would you give your son a biscuit as a reward then, just as he reaches for it, pull it back, shake salt onto it and then return it for him to eat? So why would you effectively do that with praise?

- sarcasm is said to be the lowest form of wit

- if you see it as harmless fun, reflect on the essence of humour. Is making jokes at other people's expense – especially children who won't see it the same way – the only way to have fun and make others laugh?

Teachers

- sarcasm is neither an effective nor a professional tool for teachers. It should never be used as it confuses and humiliates

50 Watch out for 'I' phrases

Praise should focus more on the event or the child than on us. Once we start sentences with 'I . . .' the emphasis becomes our view of things. 'I like the way . . .' 'I'm very pleased', 'I think you could have done more to . . .' 'I was so surprised you did so well . . .', 'I am convinced everything will go well for you because you have prepared so thoroughly.' The earlier discussion of the purpose of praise highlighted such things as acknowledgement, attention and affirmation. Children love to please their parents when they are young, but as they get older they need less of their parents' pleasure and more affirmation and confirmation that they have judged things well and are on the right track, which will encourage confidence.

If a boy is hungry for praise he will find any format rewarding, including all 'I . . .' phrases, but these won't help to wean him off any unhealthy reliance on our judgement. If he starts to sense he is being manipulated or too closely monitored, he may simply ignore them all. On the other hand, phrases such as 'You did really well', 'That was a brilliant result' or 'The way you were able to reflect on that test and spot where you went wrong was impressive', are more focused on the process and are statements of fact that centre on him, not of judgement that centre on you.

Parents

- 'you are lovely as you are, *and* you're extra special to me!' is less loaded than 'I love you as you are' – especially if he has just done something to please you

- 'you handled that really well. Others might have lost their cool. Well done!' is preferable to, 'I really liked the way you handled that'

- 'you're such fun to be around' is less of a burden to carry than 'I love being around you when you're this cheerful'

- free him: focus your remarks on his ability to set about tasks well rather than offering your opinion on the outcome

Teachers

- 'you've clearly got the measure of this problem now. This was a terrific assignment and shows what you are really capable of' is more convincing than, 'I am pleased you have understood this problem and done this piece of work so well'

58 Accentuate the positive – but notice the negative

It is fine to accentuate the positive, especially when boys are young and boisterous and get into lots of scrapes and sometimes cannot help being clumsy or physical; but as they get older the negative should increasingly be noticed, not ignored. Young children make lots of mistakes either of judgement or about their physical capacity, because it is hard for them to think ahead, because rules are hard to grasp or because they get tired, fractious or need attention. We should understand and tolerate these errors that cannot really be considered 'naughty' and we should certainly not punish them. At a period of life when mistakes and accidents abound he should be allowed to start his life feeling positive, capable and confident, not cowed by constant criticism and failure.

But by the time boys reach the age of six or seven, when they can think more reflectively, it is important that the negatives are noted and addressed and positives are kept real: in proportion both to their prevalence and to any particular achievement. The phrase, 'accentuate the positive' means, essentially, to emphasise good behaviour and to make it conspicuous, but that does not mean we should ignore outrageous behaviour or go overboard with overdone exaggerations when the event is modest.

knows it. These can all have counterproductive consequences that are explored in this chapter.

The dangers that are associated with the wrong kind of attention, be it indiscriminate praise or constant criticism, include perfectionism (explored in Chapter Ten), stress-inducing pressure, burn-out and opting out and, perhaps curiously, feelings of low self-worth. We might intend that our son feel pride and satisfaction, but this is not guaranteed. These outcomes, admittedly, lie at the extreme end; signs of interim difficulty or more serious trouble ahead can include secretiveness, mild cheating and copying of other people's work and learned helplessness.

The characteristic common to all the mistakes reviewed here is placing our concerns and desires before our son's feelings and wishes: a failure to treat him as an autonomous human being. Each child should, then, be allowed to be who he is and not be compared to anyone else or used by us as a vehicle to make good any missed opportunities of our own that we may now regret. He should be put in charge of his growth as much as possible, given the freedom to say no or stop and be offered every opportunity to do well for his own pleasure, not simply to please us. Parents often need to step in and help a child over a sticky patch, for example not understanding some maths or getting disenchanted with their progress on a musical instrument and wanting to give up; but when he has overcome the problem we should withdraw, allowing him from then on to set his own pace and direction.

60 Don't swamp him with your success

Acorns seldom grow under the great oak.

If we want our son to be able gradually to recognise when he's done well and be open about his pleasure in his accomplishments rather than rely on us for warm words, we can set an example by describing occasions when things go well for us. However, it is possible for parents to go too far and swamp their sons with their success. It is important to leave room for him to feel that small advances are worthwhile and valuable and to avoid implying that each child has to excel to fit in – or suffer derision or rejection.

Where parental success is paraded, it can create an impossible act to follow. Though many sons follow in their father' or mother's footsteps and are happy to do so, legions of others get put off by the anticipated competition and feel intimidated by any expectation to match their achievement. The best gauge of balance in the matter is whether we suggest we are better as a person for our success and feel superior, which is dangerous. If, on the other hand, we explain it as the result of hard work, luck and embracing opportunity, we are less likely to arouse complex reactions, resentments and fears.

knows it. These can all have counterproductive consequences that are explored in this chapter.

The dangers that are associated with the wrong kind of attention, be it indiscriminate praise or constant criticism, include perfectionism (explored in Chapter Ten), stress-inducing pressure, burn-out and opting out and, perhaps curiously, feelings of low self-worth. We might intend that our son feel pride and satisfaction, but this is not guaranteed. These outcomes, admittedly, lie at the extreme end; signs of interim difficulty or more serious trouble ahead can include secretiveness, mild cheating and copying of other people's work and learned helplessness.

The characteristic common to all the mistakes reviewed here is placing our concerns and desires before our son's feelings and wishes: a failure to treat him as an autonomous human being. Each child should, then, be allowed to be who he is and not be compared to anyone else or used by us as a vehicle to make good any missed opportunities of our own that we may now regret. He should be put in charge of his growth as much as possible, given the freedom to say no or stop and be offered every opportunity to do well for his own pleasure, not simply to please us. Parents often need to step in and help a child over a sticky patch, for example not understanding some maths or getting disenchanted with their progress on a musical instrument and wanting to give up; but when he has overcome the problem we should withdraw, allowing him from then on to set his own pace and direction.

59 Don't compare him to others

When our boys are babies, it is natural for all of us to look for similarities between our brand new infant and our partner, any siblings or other relatives, so that everyone feels he is part of the family immediately. Not long after, however, the comparisons with others can become far less benign.

Comments such as: 'Your brother would not have dreamt of behaving like that', 'Why can't you be an A student like your sister?' or 'Dylan eats everything when he comes here – why are you so picky?' can be upsetting. Those who lived with such taunts say that, far from being a spur to action, their childhood was tainted by them.

Even handing out equal praise or favourable comparisons can act as a brake. Saying, 'Jerry's the brainbox and Sam's the family athlete' may give each boy something to be proud of but limits the likelihood that either will explore their full talent in the other's special sphere. And comparisons with parents of the 'you take after me' variety can be dangerous, too. You may have been a budding musician and played in local concerts at the same age your son is performing, but let it be his achievement unsullied by inheritance. Any boy will want to be himself and not likened to anyone else.

Parents

* each child will respond in his own individual way to a situation because he is unique. Comparisons may stunt his development and undermine his confidence in himself

* make it clear there is room for more than one mathematician, pianist or soccer player in the family

* don't compare your son with how you were or what you did at his age. He is himself, not you, and you've probably glamorised the memory!

* labelling makes children resentful and can tempt them to do the opposite out of spite

Teachers

* see each child as an individual, not in the context of his family. Never compare him to a sibling to disparage, coerce or even praise work

* the most useful, and constructive, comparison to make is with his own previous work or performance

* be especially supportive of originality and creativity through which he is exploring and expressing his difference

60 Don't swamp him with your success

Acorns seldom grow under the great oak.

If we want our son to be able gradually to recognise when he's done well and be open about his pleasure in his accomplishments rather than rely on us for warm words, we can set an example by describing occasions when things go well for us. However, it is possible for parents to go too far and swamp their sons with their success. It is important to leave room for him to feel that small advances are worthwhile and valuable and to avoid implying that each child has to excel to fit in – or suffer derision or rejection.

Where parental success is paraded, it can create an impossible act to follow. Though many sons follow in their father' or mother's footsteps and are happy to do so, legions of others get put off by the anticipated competition and feel intimidated by any expectation to match their achievement. The best gauge of balance in the matter is whether we suggest we are better as a person for our success and feel superior, which is dangerous. If, on the other hand, we explain it as the result of hard work, luck and embracing opportunity, we are less likely to arouse complex reactions, resentments and fears.

Parents

- handle your successes with sensitivity. Convey surprise rather than worthiness, and attribute it to judgement, hard work and good fortune, not genius

- any significant success of yours will be evident; there'll be no need to blow your own trumpet

- don't strive to excel at everything. Doing something well enough, and sometimes not quite making it, sets a healthier example

- where two parents are successful in different fields, boys can find it harder to find their own niche. So value his particular strengths, and don't compete with one another, either!

Teachers

- when a boy struggles with a problem of understanding, it won't help him to declare that it is really very simple and then to re-explain it in the same way and at the same speed

- ask if anyone in the class is willing to describe how he made sense of the task or procedure

- underachieving boys will be motivated by the successful efforts of other strugglers, not by the success of the class star

CHAPTER 8

Bribes, Rewards and Incentives

Whenever parents of boys get together they often swap stories about their sons' laziness and disorganisation – in relation to anything, but especially to finishing school projects or homework before the looming deadline. Boys seem less switched on by academic work than girls, would much prefer to be outside kicking balls and are generally inclined to leave everything until the last minute. Many seem totally unconcerned by personal untidiness and are indifferent to the state of their bedrooms. We can tear our hair out with frustration and become desperate in our search for opportunities to change their ways – which we inevitably see as barriers to achieving success.

The tactic so many parents resort to in order to nudge their sons into action is offering a bribe. That's what most people call them but they are more correctly to be described as inducements, in the form of incentives and rewards. A bribe is something offered to persuade someone to do something illegal or wrong, whereas what we generally offer is an incentive to persuade our child to undertake something legal and desirable – and, usually, in his own interest – that otherwise he would not do. Perhaps we use the term 'bribe' because we feel some guilt about what we're doing, it is seen as a last resort and we would prefer that it was not necessary.

Incentives and rewards can work well but they can either lead to problems or become a problem more directly. They must be used very carefully, especially as boys grow older. When they are young, tactics such as star charts and stickers that mark progress can help impatient youngsters with short-time horizons see their progress represented visually and help boisterous, impulsive boys control their strong desires. But even five-year-olds can get cheeky and argue about whether a particular target had or had not been reached or debate how many stars a notable success deserved. The truth is that we often use incentives to engineer a particular outcome that is our priority. If overused, boys can end up bored with the game, feeling entangled by the rewards or affronted that we don't trust them to manage any challenge on their own, making them question our belief in them.

There is no obvious age after which rewards and incentives are best avoided altogether. It is more important to consider each child's personality and maturity, the problem at hand and how rewards have been used and with what success in the past. However, it is true that the older children get and the closer they get to college and work, the more they need to trust their inner resources and rely on self-motivation.

61 Be clear about the purpose

I don't want any money to make me practise my trumpet. If I wanted to do it more often, I'd do it anyway! (12)

Incentives come in various forms and send various messages. There is the 'sweeten the pill' incentive, which we use to show we realise that something is difficult. We might say, 'I can see that you might run out of steam because this is quite a challenge. When you're finished, I'll give you something to show I appreciate what you've done.'

There is the 'kick up the butt' incentive that says, in effect, 'I'm not sure you'll do it without something to tempt you.' For example, you might offer him £100 if he manages to reach the age of sixteen without smoking.

There is also the negative or threatening incentive. Instead of offering some prize, the inducement is to avoid experiencing an outright penalty or even simply not receiving something they would otherwise have. A parent might say: 'Unless you improve your exam results, I won't pay for your driving lessons like I did for your brother' or 'If you don't stop plaguing your sister, I'll take away all your action men.'

Parents

* remember, boys don't like to be pushed and pulled. Think carefully whether you really need to offer an incentive or if there is an alternative approach that may be more suitable, such as showing interest in a project and offering to hear a daily progress report

* consider the importance of the particular outcome or target in question. If it marks a crucial turning point or if something important hangs on it, there may be more reason to ensure he does his very best

* ask whether he wants or needs to have the added boost of a reward or incentive. He could now be old enough to realise this event is important and meet the challenge without help

Teachers

* think whether any incentive you offer will help him to do his best, or whether it is to raise your overall results and personal ranking

62 Rewards are more effective as surprises

My Dad doesn't often praise me so it really means something when he does. But as soon as he does, I spot the opportunity and try to get some money out of him. I usually succeed! (15)

A reward can be agreed in advance as an incentive, or it can be offered afterwards, produced as a surprise in recognition of our appreciation. Rewards are most helpful and enjoyable if they are not announced in advance, for two reasons. Given in this way, they not only avoid any unpleasant negotiation about whether the suggested reward is big enough but also reduce the chance that any boy will intentionally under perform in order to continue to benefit.

My grandmother, brought up over a century ago, used to warn all of us grandchildren, 'I want doesn't get.' It was a typical Edwardian homily, designed to warn children against covetousness. Surprises aren't dangled beforehand and are therefore more spontaneous and far less open to manipulation by either side.

Parents

- keep it as a genuine surprise. A financial reward that is prised out of you afterwards is not a surprise – unless you are! Praise is a form of reward. We generally reject the practice of double punishment, so why should we be so open to double rewards?

- in order to retain our gesture as a surprise, it follows that we cannot produce rewards too often

- surprises do not have to cost money. But the more toys and goods children possess, the harder it can be to find simple ways to please them. Examples could include cooking together, letting him use something of yours that he covets or staying up later one weekend

Teachers

- giving surprises to individual students could lay a teacher open to favouritism. However, activities which students enjoy, such as having extra time on the computer, drawing on the board or being asked to run errands during lesson time, can be offered as a surprise reward

63 Keep targets manageable: ask, can he realistically deliver?

Children like to work with adults who have confidence in them and ask them to stretch themselves, because that is when they give of their best and make progress. Doing well when the challenge is easy is neither exciting nor rewarding. But challenges must be set to tempt children to develop themselves, not put them off because they are overambitious and feel threatening. A target set too high is as unhelpful as one set too low.

We know that a target or expectation is realistic when the boy involved agrees that it is achievable. If his view is more pessimistic than ours, he may reject the objective and the reward before he starts. We should never set our child up to fail. If goals appear to him consistently unrealistic the reward will be never be earned, which could lead either to a disenchanted and more self-doubting child who then refuses to engage at all, or to a heated argument about how close he got and what other recognition he might deserve given the advance he did achieve.

Parents

* ask him what he thinks he can handle

* help him to devise clear plans to meet his goal

* if he seeks an easier target, start there and work up. Self-belief is so important to longer-term striving that it must be securely in place

* boys tend to overestimate their ability and do not usually aim low to get an easier ride. If he is pessimistic, it could signify fragile confidence

* encourage him to mix short and longer-term goals

Teachers

* make sure the goal, deadline and expectations are clear

* help boys to assess whether the conditions have been met, and face the consequences if not

* if you detect overconfidence, ask for a detailed study plan – don't say he won't make it

* don't constantly move the goal posts. Ask whether he's ready for the next challenge or needs some time for everything to sink in

64 Reward him with your presence, not presents

Grandma always comes with little gifts for us, but I still prefer grandpa because he takes the time to talk to us and he seems nicer and kinder. (7)

Rewards are used, typically, as a sign that we appreciate what our son did and to encourage him. Another good reason for using rewards is that they give children little boosts along the otherwise endless journey that is growing and learning.

Children seem naturally materialistic. They cotton on very quickly to how much things cost and are hawkish as they watch and assess whether a sibling or, especially, step-sibling gets better gifts than he does. But they are also hard-wired to detect insincerity or superficial gestures, as indicated in the quote above. They know how easy it is for many – though not all – parents to buy something. The best way to show that we truly appreciate his effort is to put some effort into our gesture, which means sharing our scarcest resource: time. Our time with him will genuinely encourage him; will demonstrate genuine appreciation, regard and approval and has infinite, not specific, value.

Parents

- depending on his age, watch him doing something he enjoys, sit with him while he eats, chat as he falls asleep, give him a lift to a friend's house or play a game

- quiet time together can be as important as action packed time. Turn your phone off!

- give more generously of your time if there have been any problems or family difficulties recently as he may be unsettled and will almost certainly need you more

- if you're a non-resident parent, after he's had a big success, make a special effort to keep any promise to visit or go out

Teachers

- find a moment to have a special quiet conversation that details his achievement and shows you are interested in and value him as an individual

- show a personal touch by relating the current work to something he wrote previously

- point out what this good piece of work means for his future potential

65 Let him help to choose the treat or incentive

This will lessen the possibility that he may see the incentive as a surreptitious attempt by us to control him as it is a celebration on his terms.

If we choose the treat, we have to guess what he would like, and we might get it wrong – missing something either obvious or an as yet undisclosed passion. If he helps to choose the treat, it need not stop it from being a nice surprise. After a pleasing outcome, we can say he deserves a treat and he can help to select it, not forgetting to give some guidance as to the appropriate scale of the event.

During the treat, he can feel like a king, having special influence and attention for a short while, which will contrast strongly with his daily diet of school when he has to fall into line and be one of a very large crowd.

Parents

- the choice of treat will necessarily vary according to a boy's age. It could be a little toy, some sweets, an extra story at bedtime, something that relates to his personal passion or hobby, choosing the destination for a special trip out, to watch a DVD just with you or with the whole family at the weekend or the choice of menu for a celebratory meal at home or out

Teachers

- there is less scope for choice in a classroom context, but rather than determine what the treat should be, if there is some scope for choice it should be offered

66 Money talks . . . back, so take care if you use it!

Children often argue about the size of the reward they deserve and push for more. What was intended as a generous gesture can degenerate into a battle of wits and power. 'I'll do it for £10, not for only £5' is a not unfamiliar cry in households where money talks loudly and is used to ensure parental will prevails. Even small children can barter over, for example, the appropriate payment for being good at the dentist.

To negotiate every penny is an obvious way to take control in a situation in which a boy senses financial manipulation. And if money is always accorded value as a reward, it may also become something a boy could desire strongly – and take – if he ever feels ignored and resentful.

Adolescent boys may be especially prone to cadge and raise the stakes with their mums. If they associate masculinity with power and power with money, which many boys do, they're more likely to want to beat their mum at the money game than any dad who plays it.

Parents

• if you hear, 'My friends have all been given £100 for doing well' don't automatically cough up. His real reward is discovering later that life's best rewards are rarely financial

• lack of money may be a suitable temporary excuse – but when any appears he'll be there, hand held out

• we might give something freely but recipients often ask why

• where money talks, it implies: spending is best; money buys influence; money matters more than time

• when it talks back, it can say: easy come, easy go; I'm not that biddable; I reject your money *and* you!

Teachers

• ask for students' views about the value of money as a reward in class discussion time

• point out that the more money children receive via financial rewards, the less they need: unless the amount rises, the incentive becomes progressively devalued

• reflect on how much you value your job because of or despite the money paid

67 Don't let money become the family's emotional currency

Mum and I had a huge falling out yesterday. She felt so guilty about it she took me out today and bought me a load of new computer games. (17)

No boy should ever feel that the bigger the present or the more money he is given, the more he is loved. Love cannot and should not be measured by price-tags. How much you love a child should never become linked to how much money you are prepared to spend on him. Where effort, commitment and love become closely equated with money and costly gifts, children can ask for ever bigger gifts and use emotional blackmail to get them.

This occurs when gifts are used to fill emotional or time gaps in relationships, when they are purchased either to say sorry or to assuage guilt. Of course all dads and mums like to buy a little gift after a trip away, but if it stops being a surprise and becomes an expectation and lever, we have to take stock. Any complaint on the lines that something more was expected because the trip had been a long one will show it is time to think afresh about how we make up for any time they miss with us.

Parents

* when financial rewards become emotional currency, children can think: 'Prove you're really pleased by giving more', or 'I did it anyway, but hey, let's lay on some guilt and see what happens!'

* stand up for yourself: don't let him exploit your love and ensure he knows, through the little things that you do and say, that you love him without proving it through giving presents

* if you feel guilty about frequent absence, talk to him directly about how sad this makes you and phone him as regularly as you can at an agreed time so he knows he is 'kept in mind'. Presents will then be less necessary

Teachers

* where boys are used to relationships at home that are conditional and based on trading, they may try the same with you. Understand where this might come from and be quiet and firm rather than angry

* remember the theory: the key to safe striving is to ensure that motivation is self-generated, not created by someone else playing on guilt or applying undue pressure

68 Focus on internal, not external rewards

Where motivation rests upon extrinsic guilt or pressure, there is less sense of self-determination. Howard Hall, Professor of Sport and Exercise Psychology, De Montfort University.

Psychological theory distinguishes between 'intrinsic' and 'extrinsic' rewards. Extrinsic rewards are those that exist outside the child, for example, money, toys, new clothes or perhaps the present of a pet. The Concise Oxford Dictionary defines extrinsic as not belonging to, not essential.

Internal, or intrinsic, rewards, by contrast, belong naturally. They lie inside each of us as positive thoughts and experiences and can be understood as essential. Examples of internal rewards are pride and pleasure; a satisfied curiosity or a sense of mastery and capability; or feeling fit, healthy and agile. Rewards are usually posed to offer encouragement and increase motivation, yet we know the most effective motivation is self-motivation. We all have to learn to do things because we want to, because we enjoy the self-satisfaction that usually flows from effort, progress and achievement. Boys need to learn to acknowledge and value these feelings and consider them sufficient reward.

Parents

* when something goes well, ask him how he feels, so he learns to 'read' and acknowledge the internal benefits of making an effort and doing himself justice

* external rewards depend on others; they pale as they become predictable and eventually become mere tokens of success. To remain an effective incentive, they have to increase

* internal rewards, by contrast, are within each person's control. If the pleasure of success fades, he simply raises the target

Teachers

* try to ensure that each boy understands and feels comfortable inside with the mark given or comment made and that he has learned something

* make sure the benefit is doing well, not simply receiving the accolade or bonus points. The older boys get, the more they like to gamble with manipulative games with rewards, and they may get hooked

69 If rewards backfire, drop them

Rewards and incentives may backfire for several reasons. A boy may simply refuse to accept them; he may argue endlessly about the nature of the reward or he may go so far but stop just short of the agreed achievement threshold and still demand the reward. If any tactic is no longer working or has turned sour, how should we respond?

The first action is to stop using rewards altogether, rather than trying to devise another that may work better. The next step is to reflect on why this strategy has become problematic. It could be that he wants to show that he doesn't need them. He might be rebelling against being treated like a puppet and want more autonomy and control in his life. It may be that his self-confidence has taken a tumble for some reason and he has become frightened of failing so he is no longer trying. It is also quite possible that he has got too big for his boots and is just trying it on.

Boys will give of their best when the atmosphere around them is emotionally uncluttered and they feel stimulated by a sense of personal growth, self-discovery and autonomy. However, boys are unlikely to feel in command or free when they feel pulled and pushed by other people's targets or expectations.

Parents

- indicate you are pleased to drop the use of rewards because you prefer to rely on trust

- make clear your confidence that he can and will deliver, for his own benefit and future

- if you need to, remind him, firmly, of any agreement and restate that you assume it will be adhered to

- from about the age of ten, invite him to list the arguments in favour of working and trying hard and the downside of letting things slip

- he will make the effort when he knows he can say his piece and is respected

Teachers

- rewards systems have to be consistent throughout any school. If the system does not seem to work with individual students, think more deeply about the possible explanation. Consider the experience of colleagues and brainstorm potentially more effective and flexible approaches, such as making specific tasks easier (fewer spellings to learn) or a quiet place to do homework in school with you or a colleague present to help him concentrate

- it is through having responsibility that children find out about themselves. Put him in charge of as much of his learning, assessment and class tasks and chores as possible

70 Channel competition safely

Boys in general have a stronger competitive urge. They are pack animals who like to jostle to be top dog if they see a possible chance. They are on the look out for potential competitors and will often work hard in secret to trounce one who is a particular threat to their latest hoped-for triumph, be it at conker fights or on the ice rink, even if the contender is a best mate. Their competitive urge is seductive as it may produce excellent results in the short term.

Research shows that where either parents or teachers set up competitions to secure improvement, the outcome is an anxious child. Any child who feels that something important hangs on the result of any test is more likely to experience pre-test nerves and go to pieces either then or later if there is a disappointing result. They may also realise their success or knowledge is shallow and feel uncomfortable about taking it seriously. Adults can harness boys' competitive instincts more safely and to better effect if they encourage a boy to compete against himself, striving to improve on his last best effort. Where the aim is to beat others the outcome is far less certain, for the competitors will also be trying hard to improve.

Parents

* it is better to identify a specific goal – 'Try to improve on your chemistry lab work' – than a general one – 'Go for an A this time'

* don't fuel competition between brothers and sisters. Each child needs to be successful in his own way, and accepted unconditionally for who he is

* fun competitions are fine. 'See if you can beat me to the top of the stairs' is a great way to get him on the way to bed

Teachers

* research shows that when competition is a main teaching tool, children become anxious

* encourage children to perform to improve, not impress, and give them feedback so they can see any progress made

* the use of co-operative, rather than competitive games, can show how much fun can be gained from simply joining in and exercising one's wits

CHAPTER 9

Using Praise to Encourage Learning and Behaviour

It would not be surprising if many readers turned to this chapter first. People often seek guidance when they feel things are going off-track. In terms of what presents as a problem to parents, school performance and behaviour are the two big ones. Praise, encouragement and positive feedback are especially valuable and effective in these two areas, and far more likely to produce happier and more self-directed children than punishment, harsh criticism or humiliation. They are also the areas in which parents can find themselves in difficulty, despite using a range of 'positive' and apparently recommended inducements, without really understanding why. It is for this reason that learning and behaviour are addressed at this point in the book, for it is important that the general principles of effective praise and some of the pitfalls of praise are absorbed before seeking answers to any immediate problem. It is important to be clear about the best ways to get the best from our children, especially when they are trying to gulp down the fresh air of freedom.

But first, a few words about both discipline and learning. The better these are understood, the easier it will be able to keep feedback and attention positive and constructive.

Learning is an emotional activity and a very complex process. It involves far more than a child simply opening his mind and receiving the knowledge being presented by the teacher, because his state of mind inevitably influences his willingness and capacity to take in information. When children struggle at school there are often several complex explanations. Difficult life events, including bullying, can distress, distract and preoccupy children so they're unable to concentrate. These same events may threaten children's self-belief because they often introduce uncertainty and powerlessness, which make children less willing to take the risks that learning entails. Panic freezes the mind and we also know that when we anticipate that something will be hard to learn, information can appear jumbled and incomprehensible. Learning and striving can arouse a range of fears: of incompetence, of failure, of reprimand and ridicule. Children are agents of their own learning. Rather than be forced to absorb information and then receive the 'gift' or reward of positive feedback, he can be offered scope to decide and say *how* best he learns, *when* he is ready to pull out the stops or *whether* he needs tokens of appreciation.

Discipline should also foster self-restraint and self-discipline. Boys shouldn't have adult requirements ruling all of their time. We set them clear guidelines early on to keep them safe and to create calm and predictability so they can feel secure. As they grow older, boys must be encouraged to judge situations for themselves and reflect on both the reasons for any disappointing behaviour and the consequences – any harm or distress caused to property or people. Eventually, they must develop their own values and manage their own study patterns and behaviour. Parents and others will encourage this if they reward reflection and responsibility and treat compliance more as an expectation.

71 Success is always relative

I had a greater sense of achievement from finishing 73rd in the national school championships aged fourteen than from coming sixth in the 10,000 metres in the 1972 Olympics which I was expected to win. It was a disaster for me. But I tried to hang on to the positive view that I was sixth best in the world. David Bedford, former 10,000m World Record Holder and now Race Director of the London Marathon.

It is important to realise that what might be a small, unremarkable step forward for one boy can be a significant mark of progress for another, and a successful result for someone who needs to work hard to do well may be a disappointing one for someone else who rides challenges easily and is capable of better. No one should be denied his parents' pleasure just because someone with greater talent was in the line-up to outshine his personal effort.

In school, children are viewed as learners and are judged and differentiated by academic ability. At home we must see our son in the round and as multi-talented; always offer a sense of hope and help him develop the self-respect necessary to acquire a positive self-image even if academic excellence is not his strong point.

Parents

* every boy learns and develops in a different way and takes a different amount of time. 'He's a late developer' may be the truth, rather than a convenient, embarrassed cover-up response to sceptical friends or relatives

* remember that stressful experiences can put learning on hold; and everyone needs times when they tread water rather than surge forward

* ask him whether it felt good to him. If it did and he's not pretending, that's good enough

* if your friends' children are apparently doing better than yours, avoid feeling competitive – yours will still be lovely as they are

Teachers

* consider each piece of work as a good or less good one *for them at this moment,* not in relation to the standard you ultimately expect

* whole class praise is good from time to time so everyone feels the benefit

72 Match the applause to the achievement

Oh good job, Danny! I love how you are sitting quietly at the table! Everyone, put your hands together for a little clap!

'Say it enthusiastically' is a mantra adopted by many parenting and management gurus and thence by parents. Of course, it is undoubtedly better to sound pleased than to describe pleasure with a deadpan expression and flat voice; however, the fervour espoused by many can go too far in the other direction and not only sound fake but also create too much tension around the requirement to continue to deserve the accolades.

If praise is about appreciation, and appreciation involves estimating the worth of something, we need to match the applause to the achievement.

Parents

- encouragement includes waiting quietly and patiently while a child works out how to do something – it shows trust that he'll manage

- saying something's great before it has been achieved is false and can imply there is pressure to get it right. However, showing appreciation of endeavour thus far suggests that that is good enough

- children feel pride and pleasure, not when they receive phoney feedback about their brilliance, but when they know they worked hard and have something significant to show for it

Teachers

- ask a student how he would like a good piece of work acknowledged other than with your written comment, if at all

- accumulate small achievements to justify a bigger splash of recognition. Three in one week or in one term could earn different rewards

- for young boys, a week or even a day is long enough. Older boys can relate to improvements over a longer period

73 Praise friendship and caring qualities too

A UNESCO report, *International Commission on Education for the Twenty-first Century*, published in 1996, identified four kinds of learning: learning to know; learning to live together; learning to be; and learning to do.

Schools focus mostly on learning to know and it is what boys know, or rather seem not to know, that upsets parents most. Yet friendship and caring qualities are also important, and if boys can work in collaboration with friends they can gain great insight and broaden their awareness from pooling ideas and approaches.

Boys seem to have more finely-honed competitive instincts and often prefer to work on their own than with fellow classmates in order to gain some distinction. However, in the adult working world teamwork is highly valued, so boys need to overcome their reluctance. At a time when it is important to their sense of masculinity to be successful and all-knowing, they may feel more exposed in group work because others will see if they can't grasp something or have no suggestions to contribute.

Parents

• having opportunities to work with friends, even if they gossip and seem to be 'off task' some of the time, can benefit a boy's learning through enhancing his language, social and communication skills

• learning is inevitably a social activity. It never happens in a vacuum. It always involves listening, interacting with a teacher, responding to peer and teachers' expectations and 'self' assumptions that are so often clarified in reference to others. Social confidence can encourage more confident work

Teachers

• if you have class awards, don't forget humour or other social attributes

• try to encourage boys to feel comfortable in group-based projects

• 'groupthink' is greater than the sum of its parts. Demonstrate through an exercise that ideas can develop and strengthen when people work together

74 Let the teacher do the teaching

My seven-year-old son enjoyed writing at home, creating well-punctuated, long stories. When he brought some schoolwork home, I was shocked at the contrast and how little care he'd taken. Instead of telling him off and pointing out his mistakes, I went to the teacher to discuss why he might be working so differently at school.

When young children are proud of something they have done, of course they want to show it to us. Rather than burst their bubble of confidence with critical comments, we should aim to appreciate the piece of work and accept that they are pleased with it. If we spot something wrong or something we felt could have been done better – as we're almost bound to being adult – we have to think carefully about how and whether to say anything. It is, essentially, for the teacher, who knows the standard expected for our child's age, to do the teaching.

If he asks us to check it over, we can be more straightforward, but first having commented positively on something we liked about the work and having checked he is ready to hear any suggestions for changes. Some children will be happy to have another go at it; others may decide they will leave it as it is – that is their choice.

Parents

* get too critical and he won't let you near to help at all

* avoid changing anything or adding finishing touches as he'll no longer see the work as his

* only the teacher can know what to expect from a boy of his age, what is really being tested in the homework, or what's best for him to learn next

* if there is a big difference between what he produces at home and in class, consult rather than berate the teacher. The problem could be a boisterous friend, boredom, disruptive classmates or feeling different if he does his best

Teachers

* parents who complain are parents that care. Go easy on them and try not to take it personally

* guidance for parents on helping with homework issued at the start of the academic year may help to keep the ground clear

75 Every day can't be judgement day

I don't like to punish any boy in my class. If someone is failing and falling behind, I deal with it by giving them personal attention. There is nothing like a one-to-one session to help iron out difficulties and make someone feel valued and hopeful. But I would do it very quietly and not announce to the class that this is what I felt was needed.

If our bosses were to check us over each day and give us daily marks out of ten, we'd end up ragged and neurotic. That's how children must feel when they are regaled with constant expressions of pleasure and disapproval. They will find it hard to find that necessary private space when they feel they are being watched incessantly. One teenager told me it was his mother's carping, alternated with squeals of delight according to each day's events, that led him to clam up when she asked what had happened at school.

Parents

• encouragement contains no judgement. It leaves him free to take himself forward in his own way

• use encouraging comments to help him to feel you're appreciating rather than judging:
- you've put so much effort into that!
- I wish I'd done such good things at school
- it's hard for you but you will crack it

• take away any guilt or shame he might feel if he anticipates judgement: 'That wasn't at all like you. Let's put it behind us and start again tomorrow'

Teachers

• make earning any 'good work' stickers fun

76 Show interest but don't be intrusive

One mum who had a very high-powered job said she was not going to attend the parent consultation session at her son's school because she considered it up to them to get the teaching right. She wasn't interested to hear what she could do – that was what she was paying them for.

How wrong she was! Of course we should be interested in our child's progress and happiness in all areas of development at school. For all schoolchildren, school is almost as important as their family; for older children, it is probably more important.

But we have a dilemma. After the age of eight or so, children relish school as the place where they can disappear from the often intense gaze of their parents' constant scrutiny. They need some privacy. Their need for praise from us becomes offset gradually by their need for autonomy. When boys want our appreciation, they'll tell us all we need to know.

Parents

• ask open-ended questions that allow him to withhold detail. 'Did anything good or bad happen today?' not 'Who did you play with and what happened?' And start by talking about *your* day

• ask casually about marks gained. 'That tricky maths test, how did it go down?' rather than 'What mark did you get, will I be pleased?'

• if you overhear talk of a difficulty, offer to discuss it but don't demand details

• make sure questions are genuine, not designed to find out something else

• take an interest in his work but don't take it over and do it for him

Teachers

• show interest in his personal passions or hobbies but step back if he seems uncomfortable about it

• his family experiences influence a great deal. It is important to understand and acknowledge these but also to treat anything you learn about with respect as many children prefer this information to remain private

• at parent-teacher events and in newsletters, stress the important role that parents can play in encouraging schoolwork and being interested in any developments at the school

77 Give him hope

Getting there is as important as arriving and along the road there should always be hope. Most boys give up either because they have been told over and over again that they are a hopeless case or because they doubt their capacity to do well for other reasons. The message many hear is demoralising and undermining: 'You won't if you don't . . .'; 'You will never if you carry on . . .' or 'You're a born loser, never been any good at . . .' Rather than risk further failure and have salt rubbed in already torn egos, many will decide not to try. Labels tend to stick and act as straightjackets, preventing boys from escaping from the negative destiny that someone has assumed for them.

What boys need to hear are far more hopeful messages that will not only boost their self-belief but also make any target seem manageable and easy to keep up once achieved. 'Of course this is hard, but just take it one step at a time and you'll have no problem'; 'You've managed to stay close and not run off from the vegetable section all the way to the meat. It's not so far now to the checkout. Did you think you think it would be this easy? I knew you could do it!' for example.

Parents

* remind him of past successes so he thinks positively and believes in himself

* if success appears unfamiliar or scary and seems to carry heavy responsibilities for continuing in the same vein, it may be easier for a boy to remain the devil he knows

* if he sets himself a goal that he's failed to complete before, such as to cover his bedroom wall with posters and photos from magazines, don't remind him of the past failure. Greet each resolution as a first and stay positive

* motivation is grounded in hope and experience

Teachers

* sarcasm and ridicule usually puncture hope. Don't use them

* make sure that his hope is grounded in a practical reality – help him to put together a plan

* break the challenge down into small, manageable chunks and remind him of difficulties he has previously overcome

78 Boys like to keep a bit of themselves back

Boys like to keep a bit of themselves back, so their work is rarely perfect. They like to take the short cuts, prefer to answer their science questions in incomplete sentences and not bother too much about neatness. We're used to that. I don't like to squeeze much more out of them if they've clearly understood the work.

The views above were expressed by an experienced secondary school science teacher. Whether it relates to male pride or an extra sensitivity that boys have to power struggles with parents, boys seem to feel they give too much of themselves away when they do everything exactly as asked by an adult. Whether it is managing their bedrooms or behaviour at home or their homework for school, boys like to persuade themselves that they're still in control, that they haven't sold their soul. Doing almost all of it, or doing it nearly right, is often as good as you're going to get.

Rather than force them to do it your way, to your standards resulting in a truculent youth keen to assert his will by fair means or foul, it's better to accept that enough is, indeed, enough to accept and be worthy of your appreciation.

Parents

* respect his difference. Don't try to take over his soul

* be tolerant. This 'unfinished business' approach to many tasks may also reflect boys' greater difficulty with concentrating for long periods of time

* boys may need especially to create a protective moat between themselves and successful fathers that have high expectations for their sons. Respond with empathy rather than insisting that standards must not be allowed to slip

Teachers

* be understanding of work that's not quite what you had in mind, provided it is thought through, demonstrates learning and is legible

* avoid commanding total obedience in every way. Have a joke about minor truculence and male pride

79 Two steps forward, one back

Learning anything is a strange business for it rarely happens in a predictable way or to a set pattern. Children learn, mature and develop in phases and spurts and each one will manage it in his unique way. Boys get 'eureka' moments when everything falls into place but then they can get quite scared and may want to return to the time they were more dependent and needed to rely on help. That way, they do not risk being wrong. At each stage of the advance, they can feel quite exposed. Learning, therefore, is often a case of two steps forward, one step back as the knowledge or new behaviour gets to feel normal.

In relation to behaviour, boys often need to test our reactions, to check we really have become the cooler, kinder parents and won't revert to being harsh or frightening if he slips up again. If parents ride the swells and eddies because this is understood, this is a form of acceptance and affirmation that has the same effect as giving direct praise.

We may also witness 'two steps back, three great leaps forward'. Younger children can appear to go into reverse before they make a significant developmental advance – their brains seem to take a holiday before they go full speed ahead.

Parents

* when a boy needs to tread water for a while and take time out from the pressure of eternal 'progress', he should certainly not be frowned upon or punished

* if your son seems to have 'lost it' and become confused or cannot do something he could before, wait patiently. Within a week it is likely he will have rediscovered the ability, taken a leap forward – or he will have become poorly!

* children learn by doing but they also learn by sleeping on it, imagining it, playing with the idea and thinking it through subconsciously. Don't ask for minute evidence that he is figuring it out logically, step-by-step

Teachers

* targets, assessment tests and league tables assume that every child is developing as the 'average' when each one progresses uniquely

* try to include some flexibility in the study programme

* give a flagging boy confidence that he is not stupid, merely working on the problem in his way and at his own speed

* try to convince him that he'll catch up, and impress that, like any investment, past performance is no guarantee of future outcomes!

80 Pick on one thing at a time

At my son's parent consultation evening, a number of teachers said he could do better than at present. He was performing fine in his favourite subjects, so there was nothing wrong with his working habits or brain when fired up. But instead of asking him to do each teacher's bidding, I suggested that he apply extra effort to one subject each term to keep it manageable. He felt no pressure and his work gradually improved.

Boys tend to be active and busy, which means they can find it hard to concentrate on doing the right things for a whole day. They make lots of mistakes and it is equally trying for us to monitor every move to ensure our son is obliging and obedient. He has someone constantly on his back, and our spying tactics imply we expect transgressions and don't trust him.

Everyone benefits by picking on one aspect of behaviour or schoolwork to turn around at a time. The chances of success are higher, the nagging and snooping reduces and life is more generally relaxed. Most valuable, once things have improved on the central problem, other challenging behaviour tends to disappear as a result of fewer fights, less resentment and a higher profile of praise and encouragement.

Parents

• identify the behaviour that bothers you most or the time of day that is most trying and start there. Drop the nagging about other problems until the top priority is sorted

• let him know that this is your plan, and make it seem like a fair contract: he does his bit and you do yours, which is staying cool about other matters

• for schoolwork, suggest that he works to improve one subject at a time. Don't ask him to pull out the stops on his reading and his maths, or his science and his history at the same time

Teachers

• with a challenging class, reflect upon the source of the main problem – a handful of particularly disruptive students, classroom management (because they sit and disrupt together) or teaching style (because some seem to lose interest very quickly). Pick on the most plausible explanation and unravel that problem first

• give boys who struggle clear and achievable short-term goals so they know exactly where they must focus and see the way forward. When one does well, make sure he knows exactly what he did that led to the improvement

CHAPTER 10

Avoiding the Perils of Perfectionism

Many people have become concerned that an increasing pressure to achieve and do well has led to more high flying students becoming perfectionists and 'success junkies', dependent on their regular fix of achievement and accolade, success and celebration, without which they feel incomplete. For example, in the USA, the former Dean of Harvard's undergraduate college, Harry Lewis, was openly concerned by some students' need to impress and to receive acknowledgement and rewards for everything when he wrote to students: 'You may balance your life better if you participate in some activities purely for fun . . . many of the most important and rewarding things that you do will be recorded on no piece of paper you take with you but only as imprints on your mind and soul.'

There are similar concerns in the United Kingdom over the growing pressures in competitive elite sport and the demand for perpetual progress at school. While some children seem able to survive, even thrive on, the pressures, others may develop an unhealthy level of perfectionism that conceals considerable self-doubt and distress because they pursue, sometimes impossible, goals and are never satisfied with the result.

What attitudes and support help to keep children free from turmoil and competitive anxiety? Research shows that children who aim high, do well and can sustain success in a healthy and balanced way work to their own, realistic and flexible standards and expectations. They can ride mistakes and failures and learn from them. They tend to be well organised, have uncritical parents and strive for their own benefit because they enjoy the activity. They are in control and don't feel pushed. Most important, they have a robust self-esteem that does not rely on proving themselves to others or coming top to buoy them up.

The seeds of unhealthy perfectionism take root where, in the eyes of the child, parental approval appears conditional on success; they strive to meet very high and inflexible expectations they see others hold for them; where adults take the credit for, or 'steal' any success; where no success ever seems good enough because targets are continuously raised; where constant challenge generates constant doubt about ability; and where success is lauded, failure is shunned and fear of failure is intense. In other words, perfectionist attitudes do not help children to be happy, despite the impressive achievements that often accumulate.

81 Keep all goals realistic and flexible

Everyone gets scars on the way to the stars. The tittle of a song written by Fran Landesman, jazz singer.

Parents and teachers are often tempted to ask a child to go that extra mile and are loathe to make the target easier if the child then struggles. If a problem appears, it is attitude and application that are considered the culprit, not an unrealistic target.

Research shows that being able to be flexible and to compromise on standards and targets is one of the keys to healthy striving. If a boy begins to set tough targets and beats himself up emotionally if he doesn't quite get there, encourage him to go easy. Of course it's great if he does very well but it is more important that he doesn't find himself in the stranglehold of a perfectionist straightjacket.

Parents

* never berate a boy for having not quite excelled, even as a joke

* if he is short-listed for a further test after doing well in any preliminary trial or a test, mark that as sufficient success with a surprise treat. Don't wait until the final outcome, because he has already proven that he has promise

* try to demonstrate flexibility in your own goal-setting

* don't harbour inflexible goals for your son

Teachers

* boys need firm expectations for meeting deadlines, to prevent procrastination from becoming a habit, but flexible expectations where a student has determined his own goal

* make it clear that each student achieves at a different level, and that high performance should not come at the expense of enriching leisure time or mental composure

82 Don't make approval conditional on his success

When my son was not selected to be head of his school, I felt let down and almost angry. I got really picky with him. I found myself putting him down. I'm an intelligent and successful businessman and was both horrified and ashamed that I felt this way. It just happened.

At least he admitted his feelings. This father's first reaction – of vindictive disappointment – is more common than anyone would care to accept, although his subsequent insight is far less usual. If we expect good things, it is very easy to feel disappointed and let down if they do not happen, but no child should suffer the burden of believing that success is the only way to maintain either parent's love or approval.

We might have a similar reaction if our son behaved badly on an occasion that mattered to us and we felt shown up. If we 'went cold' on him but did not actually reprimand him for a specific wrongdoing, we could be falling into the trap of reserving our approval for times when he makes us feel good.

Parents

* accept that it is not good for him to be perfect, and that every experience, including a setback, is an important stepping stone in learning and growing

* see the funny side and the alternative potential of any shortfalls

* if you find yourself being disappointed by a second best outcome, it is time to remind yourself that you are not him, and he is not you. In your mind, draw a boundary between you and him and stop living parasitically through him

Teachers

* treat all students fairly, without favouritism. Accept each one as a worthwhile individual; don't reserve your enthusiasm for the accommodating and successful ones

* show that you value a wide range of attitudes, specialist knowledge and skills. Refer to past achievements and anticipate future ones

* focus on the process as well as the outcome. How the improvement was achieved is the aspect to highlight, rather than the success itself

* encourage all students to take important decisions and responsibility for these, so each one feels trusted by you

83 Let your son take, and keep, ownership of the success

He shouldn't complain that he wasn't told about your son's great result. I agree with you. Children need to keep possession of any success and realise that it's theirs. No one should run off and tell the world, like it was their achievement and their prize. Special educational needs expert and head teacher.

Of course, our son owns his success but it is very easy to take it over and thereby take it from him. That is what we are doing when we use it to make us feel successful. We feel so thrilled by the achievement we are almost driven to run off with it and show it to all our friends by telling them. We can get enormous kudos from our children doing very well in their various activities.

But if we effectively steal his success and spread around any special news, rather than feel fulfilled, our son could be left feeling empty and bereft. He could then feel driven to replenish the success, over and over again.

Parents

• personal success should be seen as the child's property, not the parent's. You would not consider borrowing anything of his without asking, and the same courtesy should apply here

• check first whether he wishes anyone else to know, and if he would like to tell any particular person himself

• asking him not only shows you respect him and his wishes, but also makes the success unambiguously his

• devaluing something that is a success in his terms is another way of taking the achievement and pleasure away from him: 'But a third of the class got that mark. That's not so special!'

Teachers

• when schools use children's achievements to pump up their prospectuses, there is a danger that students will feel used

84 Stay in touch with his reality

Don't be arrogant enough to assume you always know what he wants and how he feels. It is important to keep talking and giving him the opportunity to discuss freely his fears and feelings, including those that could hurt or disappoint you.

He must be free to talk about shame, letting you down, always having hankered after some other activity than the one you encouraged or his fear of failure and perhaps distorted imaginings. There will be pluses to discuss, too: which aspects of his life give him the most pleasure, how he rates each of his talents or particular skills.

For example, if you celebrate a child's success, the event should suit him, not us. A ten-year-old could find it hard to relate to a hoard of neighbours or relatives descending, talking to each other and enjoying alcohol. If he is shy, as is likely, he'll probably slope off to his room – so what benefit was it to him?

Parents

* pitch the celebration at his level, not how we would mark something notable that happens to us

* take his worries seriously. Don't ignore something that saddens him

* if we refuse to see things his way, he could lose touch with himself and become merely a reflection of us

* younger children readily believe the unbelievable, such as Father Christmas and tooth fairies. They make sense of things in surprising ways. Just because we know why something has to be, it does not follow he also understands why

Teachers

* try to uncover any worries that lie behind late, 'lost' or very poor work. There could be distress at home or he could fear demonstrating his total lack of understanding so not bother at all

* appreciate that strong parental antagonism to school and study could dilute a boy's commitment to work. It is a conflicting reality for him and he's likely to struggle with the conflict

85 Talk about 'development', not 'improvement'

Boys who have the opportunity to discover new interests, talents and skills learn more about themselves and establish a pattern of self-discovery that can enrich the rest of their lives. Self-discovery is, indeed, the main purpose: only if they explore what is there in bud inside them can they discover their true potential, and experience the thrill and excitement that lies in store. The process should be one of self-development, not self-improvement.

Self-improvement implies that a boy is progressively better and cleverer than he was before. It suggests that how he was before was not 'right'; yet, to repeat, he needs to see his past as an acceptable part of him. The subtle message could be that he needs to go on getting better and improving himself, trying one new thing after another in order to remain acceptable to his parent. We should not demand that he 'fulfil his potential', because we can never know what potential he has or when it is fulfilled. Better to ask him to unpeel a layer or two of possible resistance to reveal his reserve of capability – for his own enjoyment.

Parents

* make it clear that it is the results or the technique that is improving, not his personality or 'self'

* talk about discovery, rather than improvement. 'You're discovering all sorts of new things about yourself!', 'You're discovering you can feel comfortable with maths after all', 'Did you think you could pull out those extra stops and improve your sprint time so successfully?'

Teachers

* separate the boy from the improvement. Talk about his understanding deepening, his application becoming more effective, his new inspiration or his growing skill at identifying reference materials or with a technique, rather marvelling at his 'improvement'

86 Encourage self-appraisal

Society has told boys for a very long time that they must ultimately manage on their own and the sooner they start, the better – for so long, in fact, that it could now be programmed into their brains. Boys are proud. They don't always want to do everything they are told especially if it is mothers and female teachers doing the telling. From the start of the pre-teen years and well into adolescence, boys have a tendency to disparage girls and women to establish a clearer masculine identity. If praise is not transmitted carefully, even that can be viewed with suspicion as a tool of manipulation.

The best tactic with boys is to encourage self-appraisal. Facing their strengths and weaknesses head on will not only increase realism and self-knowledge but also avoid typically male 'posturing'. It also takes the power out of praise. Parents can nonetheless offer positive support, either by reinforcing their son's individual judgements or by reflecting encouragingly at the end of the week. Of course, if he has a significant 'victory' we can be more spontaneously appreciative.

Parents

* ask, 'But what did you think of it? That's the more important test because you are the best judge'

* try to encourage him to be specific: 'You said you thought you did badly. What was it that didn't go right?' or, 'Yes, I liked what you did too. What pleased you in particular?'

* such details become the check points for assessing the accuracy or relevance of his judgement

* before his school report is due, ask him for his best guess of what will be included

Teachers

* some teachers invite their students to moderate each other's work, having first discussed which points, skills and understandings needed to be covered. The judgement any boy applies to another's work will be fresh to apply to his own

* ask any boy whom you feel is widely misjudging the standard expected how he responds to your comments on any assignment

87 Don't constantly move the goal posts

My four-year-old son was well-prepared for his inoculations at the doctor's, so much so he didn't cry at all. Amazed at such maturity, the doctor decided to give the second dose at the same time. The result was traumatic: a distressed and disconsolate child who felt let down by both mother and doctor.

Demanding schools and parents are prone to move the goal posts. As soon as one target is in sight and therefore appears easy, another more challenging one is presented to prevent any flagging of effort. Or as soon as one goal has been reached, another is put in place to maintain the momentum: 'If you can achieve that, then surely this is also within reach!' A common example of this process in action is musical instrument examinations, where having prepared for and sat one grade, the next one up, or even two up, is immediately presented as the new objective.

But boys like to decide when they undertake challenges. They have become used to computer games in which they select the level of difficulty and start again as a 'beginner' in a higher level only when top scores at a previous level fail to please. It is very empowering.

Parents

* challenges must tempt boys to discover themselves, not threaten them, put them off or make them feel inadequate until they fulfil them

* when boys take their own time to select the target, their readiness reflects their confidence

* shifting goal posts represent a broken deal. They can store up resentment, self-doubt and anxiety

* some happily amateur yet active musicians never took instrumental exams as children. Grade exams can chart progress but are not essential

Teachers

* factor in the child's view of what he can achieve and put him in control as far as is practical to reduce the pressure

* asking for perfect answers before moving someone on encourages perfectionist attitudes or boredom

88 Accept good enough success

Growing up feeling my best wasn't good enough encouraged me to become defiant and stop trying. But although I appeared no longer to care I continued to beat myself up inside for being useless.

Any boy faced with successive mirage-style targets, as discussed in the previous tip – ones that disappear as you approach, like the shimmering 'puddles' of water on hot roads on sunny days – will very likely conclude that no success is good enough. If no success, however great, is good enough, a child will never know if he is good enough; or, indeed, if he is any good at all. This is a very uncomfortable thought, so he will need to achieve more success to convince him that he is good enough and worthy of praise. Success, if sought for this reason, will not raise self-esteem or self-belief, or deepen the self-concept. At worst, it deepens self-doubt; at best it leaves someone's self-esteem vulnerable and prone to fluctuation.

Self-belief does not come from a sense that we are perfect but from the knowledge that we are good enough but have more to give.

Parents

* lead him when he's ready. For success to feed through constructively to self-worth, a boy needs time to absorb the achievement, be sure he can repeat it and make it part of his identity. Only he can know when he is ready

* being pushed to move on too soon generates considerable anxiety, a noted characteristic of perfectionists who feel driven by others

* good enough success is not a cop-out, accepting second best or laziness. It is the result of honest (though perhaps not top gear) striving that produces real progress, and is the guard against either internal or external pressure

Teachers

* let all success be good enough, at least for a time, including your own

* ask your students when they are ready to make an extra push to raise their scores, enter a competition or jump a grading or group

* untidy work can be considered good enough if the content is sound. Boys do cut corners, use less full sentences and hurry their way through, caring less about presentation

89 Taking reasonable risks is important

Research shows that boys begin life being more inclined to take risks than girls. They think ahead less so are bolder and less cautious: they jump straight into things without thinking, get into more scrapes and therefore can end up being told off more. This bravado encourages boys to leave things to the last minute, protected by their conviction that 'it'll go just fine on the night'.

The ability to take risks is important, for learning is a risky business. Coming down hard when he's risked something and got it wrong or, even worse, punishing that error, could lead him to avoid larger risks.

Boys with perfectionist tendencies set very high standards for themselves. Fear of falling short tempts some to self-handicap to avoid anxiety, consciously or unconsciously. A boy may procrastinate and put things off until it is too late, aim ridiculously high to guarantee failure or too low so the result means nothing. Opting out is another possibility, and some develop inexplicably lethargy (ME), strange pains or eating disorders, any of which provides a welcome excuse to exit the rat race.

Parents

* make it safe to make mistakes

* talk honestly about any mistakes you might have made in the past and any you make now

* if you have taken a risk in any field, discuss with him why, the downsides and whether and how it paid off

* adventurous play that incorporates a measure of planned risk or that confronts the unexpected is helpful to learning

* promote self-direction. Don't become so involved and protective that he is never exposed to risk and therefore becomes risk averse

Teachers

* if you make a mistake, be open and honest about it

* raise class awareness of differing attitudes to mistakes by initiating a discussion. Observe any gender patterns, and talk about this

* boys love class games and quizzes in which they can prove their cleverness – or expose their limitations. Girls are often too timid to enjoy them. Invite students to reflect upon what winning, losing or participating means to them

* boys with low self-belief have neither the courage to take chances nor the confidence to change

90 Don't ignore or punish failure

Parents are often advised to encourage children by ignoring mistakes and focusing on what they do well. This helps very young boys who find it hard to control their bodies and feelings when they are taking the first steps in learning and are too young to live within wall-to-wall rules. However, as they mature they must learn to be honest about the quality and effect of their work and behaviour. To continue to disregard failures while celebrating successes suggests that failure is shameful and must be avoided: a view typical of perfectionists.

Failure is not something to be shunned. It provides factual and neutral information on what went wrong, what has not been understood fully and on what needs to be changed to get it right next time. The experience of failure becomes shameful to a child only where he has invested his self-worth in doing well, or where a parent seems to rely for their own sense of satisfaction and happiness on their son's success. Making mistakes is an inevitable and essential part of learning and can demonstrate that learning is taking place, pushing back the frontiers of knowledge and understanding.

Parents

* respond sensitively to set backs. Neither punishment nor trivialisation is a helpful reaction to disappointments

* help him to take responsibility for any failure. Make him move beyond the cover of feeble excuses to be clear about what went wrong

* see failure as neutral and don't rub his nose in it or tease him. Discourage him from taking it too personally

* if his failures become your personal shame or his successes lift you from gloom, you make it harder for him

* fortify his heart, don't thicken his skin

Teachers

* boys can see failure as a challenge to their masculine power and dominance. Help to take the shame out of any failure and clarify the lessons to be learned

* hear his side of the story

CHAPTER 11

Praise and You

Having spoken to countless adults over the years, to people who have been successful as well as those leading less remarkable lives, it is surprising how many were quick to volunteer that their parents, and particularly fathers, never praised them. They never felt their efforts were appreciated and were left with a feeling that they were simply not good enough or not sufficiently interesting personalities to be noticed. For some it has influenced the course of their life, for they are still playing to that gallery in an effort to please even though the parent is no longer around to watch the show. It remains unfinished business; and while this urge may lead to higher achievement than a more contented childhood might have delivered, the success masks an eternal sadness, sense of being let down and an underlying restlessness.

One acquaintance, who has a high public profile, agreed that her desire to prove herself as good as her brothers in the eyes of her father had generated her need to do well and make a mark from a young age. One man who sits at the top of his profession readily acknowledged the importance of self-esteem and said he had suffered quietly all his life because his father had neither praised him nor appeared to recognise or value his talents. As a consequence, he was happy now to be able to work with young students and graduates to encourage them to strengthen their sense of self through acquiring wider experiences of which they could feel proud.

Someone who experienced difficulty at the other end of the range of parental behaviour is a young woman who showed early musical talent and was expected to meet demanding practice and performance schedules as a result to make it her career. She was praised, but grudgingly and with conditions attached. Her success was never good enough. She felt increasingly that her life was not her own and the only way to regain control was to give up. From that day, she never touched her instrument again.

It is surprising that so many people have been so honest, for adults more commonly deny the importance of the things they weren't lucky enough to have or, alternatively, state that something potentially unpleasant that did happen had no lasting ill-effect. The conclusion has to be that the impact on children, young or older, of living either without apparent parental pleasure, acknowledgement or recognition, or with parents who push too hard for their own gain is clearly profound: it is a pattern that we should ensure does not get repeated.

91 Unblock your blocks to giving praise

Many people find it very hard to give praise. Some feel uncomfortable with using the unfamiliar words; some simply do not know what to praise while others squirm with disapproval at – or are deeply sceptical about – the whole process. The most common reasons people have to justify being sparing with praise include:

- that it can easily make a boy big-headed
- that praise should be given only for 'excellence': outstanding achievement and effort beyond expectation. 'Normal' behaviour, achievement or work should not merit special attention
- that if something could be better, it should not be praised as this could encourage laziness and send the wrong messages about general standards and expectations; that a boy should be doing well in every sphere before he gets rewarded in case he takes a slide in an activity a parent thinks really matters
- that they created the success, not the boy, because they forced the study regime or paid for extra tuition, for example
- that previously it has had no impact, so they drop it

In general, fathers can be keen to maintain an edge over a son and be slow to acknowledge any academic, creative or sporting success that may threaten their hold on authority and pride.

Parents

* reflect on your childhood experiences and your current attitudes to giving and receiving praise. What has been your strongest influence?

* think hard to detect any difference in your treatment of girls and boys

* if you work outside the home, how do you praise people there, if at all? Do you have the same approach at home? If not, why not?

* give as you receive. When your son shows you affection and regard (both can be considered as praise), make sure you reciprocate

Teachers

* reflect on your past, at home and at school, and ponder on any patterns you could be repeating

* consider whether you find it easier to respond encouragingly in the classroom or at home with your own family, and think through why it might be so

92 Ask for it if you want to hear it

If you do not receive much positive feedback from family, work or friends, it is likely that you have learned to do without it. Men tend to be more self-sufficient, or like to consider themselves so, and may not even notice its absence. Women are more praisehungry in childhood and are also more likely to miss getting pats on the back as adults.

If you want to hear it, ask for it; most 'significant others' are willing to be supportive once they realise that partners or friends want some back up. Very few will refuse. Children can be encouraged to be appreciative after you have done something well, not just to be polite but as a genuine recognition of the special effort or achievement.

Those who think they can do without praise and consider it a big fuss about not very much will almost certainly find it harder to offer it to others. They may think that boys, especially, should learn to grow up less needy of other people's approval. The best way to encourage a reluctant partner to become freer with his or her appreciation towards a child of yours is to take a back route and praise and appreciate them overtly first.

Parents

* be specific: analyse what you'd like to have more of, for example appreciation of your efforts or talents or acceptance of your views and values, then go and ask for it

* children tend to take what is done for them, at any level, as 'normal parenting'. It's hard for them to see that less might be done for them, so don't be harsh about their apparent insensitivity

* it is healthier to do something because you want to (in which case perhaps you don't need big thanks) rather than to curry favour. But if you'd like your efforts appreciated, describe that bit extra that you gave. Genuine thanks grow from genuine giving

Teachers

* think which job you consider you do well and whose appreciation you would value. Then go and seek confirmation and reinforcement

* positive feedback can come from colleagues, line managers, students and parents. How might each of these show their appreciation? What might you be entitled to expect?

93 If you did something well, believe it

In a world that seems obsessed with excellence, especially achievements that deliver big financial rewards, it can be hard to feel any pride in less obvious successes – or to realise that is what they are, given their modest scale.

People at work are increasingly being encouraged to identify and acknowledge their strengths and achievements. These might be relatively minor, such as responding sensitively to a junior member of staff who came in with a problem but left with a lighter step and a plan of action. In the home environment, there's no boss to offer compliments on your efforts that day, no daily target to meet. But we have good moments and successes nonetheless, and there are hundreds of tasks to be done, with or without our children, that involve the same efficiency skills, conflict resolution, stress management, practical, communication and listening skills that we have to demonstrate in the workplace.

Looking at what we did and did well, rather than at what we did not do, and feeling pleased about it, will act as a boost and help us to be positive and encouraging with our sons and partners.

Parents

* an appreciative child is one that smiles, is happy and shows affection to you. And sometimes he actually says thanks

* sometimes a boy will bounce on you from behind as a loving gesture, so take it for what it is – don't react harshly

* if you feel uncomfortable receiving praise, learn simply to say 'thank you' and hold onto it, don't bat it back

Teachers

* if you receive good feedback from a colleague, senior manager, parent or student about something you have done, accept that it is valid. Don't squirm and claim you did not deserve it or the affirmation was uncalled for because it was just in the line of duty

94 Reward yourself

If you consider you have done something impressive, either given your starting point or because it represented a significant step towards a longer-term goal, reward yourself. Whatever is your special treat, allow yourself to have or do it.

It can be a private reward that you keep to yourself, or it could be something you choose to share with one other person. It might be sitting down with an easy-to-read trashy book, watching a film or DVD during the day, taking a long, scented bath, a drink with a friend or watching sport on TV all day one weekend.

Marking an achievement with a reward helps you to acknowledge that you got there, so you are entitled to take a break; it proves that you are not compelled always to go that one step further before you allow yourself to feel pleased; and it enables you to understand how your children might also value each small gesture of appreciation and feel their effort was worthwhile.

Parents

* think of things you might enjoy doing in any spare time, such as taking a walk or spending time in the garden. Remember these when you feel you deserve a small, or larger, treat

* the best reward is your own satisfaction; then there are no ifs and buts floating around in your head. Practise saying to yourself, 'Well done! I can be really pleased about that'

* rewards don't always have to benefit you. You can share a treat or treat someone else if that gives you pleasure

Teachers

* reflect on the times during an inevitably pressured day that you might enjoy some respite when you feel you deserve it

* remember good enough success. Making a special effort, even if things didn't go entirely as planned, is worth marking otherwise you might not try again!

95 Accept any praise given to you

If someone praises you, accept it and hold onto it. Don't squirm with discomfort or hand it back as soon as you can with the words: 'It was nothing very special', 'I'm not sure what I've done to deserve a comment like that' or 'I was going to do it anyway'. Girls and women are particularly prone to such self-denigration. They may have tried hard but they usually believe that they should have done that anyway, which makes the effort seem commonplace, not worthy of comment.

If you often feel you don't deserve any recognition or accolade and you instead feel embarrassed when someone tells you you have done well, you may imagine others feel the same, including your child. This makes it more likely you will be sparing with your praise, to protect him from the expected discomfort.

But this reticence is not helpful. Far better to change your mindset and learn to accept positive feedback with good grace when you are fortunate enough to receive it!

Parents

* practise saying 'thank you' when you are given praise, and teach your boys to do the same

* don't make a joke about giving or hearing praise until everyone in the family knows that, mostly, it is given straight and can be trusted. Only then is it safe to lighten things with a bit of fun, and then only on the odd occasion

Teachers

* if any student says, 'that was good fun!' or 'that was interesting', respond with a thank you rather than 'good'. His comment is intended as complimentary feedback, not to make you realise he enjoyed it

96 Don't compete against your son

My father was so competitive with me. He would always have to beat me at chess, even when I first started playing, and claim he knew more than me about anything. I felt he took the pleasure out of my passions, almost stole it. From the age of eleven, I rode a bike to school and lo and behold he took it up as weekend exercise. When I took up running, you can imagine the so called 'fun' competitions he arranged to prove he could run faster. It was so sad and probably meant he felt very insecure, but during my chilhood it made me feel he could never be proud of me. It also made it hard to be proud of myself.

Avoid competing against your son. Some mothers and fathers find it hard to give their children the space to become better than, more good looking than, more skilled than themselves. But growing boys need to feel respected for their achievements and to be able to feel proud, not constantly pushed into the parental shadows.

Parents

- becoming competitive is more likely to switch him off than spur him to greater effort as it could make him feel overpowered and dejected

- let him, sometimes, be better than you

- if you are competitive with him, he's more likely to be so with others

- avoid referring to your past to claim any superior edge because you will almost certainly not have remembered the time or event accurately

Teachers

- 'clever clogs' students may become irritating but never try to trip them up with difficult questions or be tempted to beat them in a competitive exchange of knowledge

97 Model respect for females

A father or father figure can help a boy to do well not just by praising him but also by expressing his respect for the professionalism of any female teacher, coach or carer, family friend or relative and, naturally, his mother. Hearing upbeat and supportive views about their capabilities, specialist knowledge and personal characteristics will help a boy to feel comfortable learning and taking advice from women.

This is especially valuable when he becomes more gender aware and thence inclined to be antagonistic to girls and older females – somewhere between the ages of eight to ten. Boys will do better and do themselves greater justice if they are able to distance themselves from macho culture which tends to present masculinity as necessarily powerful and aggressive (and anti-swot) and superior to anything female that is seen to be tainted with weakness.

Research shows that any verbal or physical abuse or intimidation directed at his mother can severely damage a boy's self-esteem, mental health and future chances in life.

Parents

- respect needs to be earned as a boy matures and becomes more discriminating. He will watch how well both parents treat others and judge whether he should give them his respect

- watch your words and reactions as you watch films or television together. Swearing, catcalls or other derogatory remarks often imply disrespect

- boys won't respect women if their mothers don't respect themselves or allow their sons to exploit them or be rude. Enforcing house rules that protect your interests is a first step

Teachers

- every school should adopt sexual harassment and anti-discrimination policies. Girls and female staff should, of course, treat their male colleagues and peers with the same respect

- gender awareness and equality of regard should apply throughout the school and in every lesson

98 Enjoy your own company and that of others

The best thing about having friends is you can assume they spend time with you because they enjoy your company. If they didn't, they wouldn't. They let you know that you are good to be around, which at times can be quite intoxicating – and of course they are also there to share your problems if you ever need them as well as providing a great source of fun.

Enjoying the company of your friends will help you to realise why it is good to enjoy the company of your son. It will make him feel valued and appreciate that he is someone who is able to give other people pleasure rather than be a source of disappointment and strife and will provide an enormous boost to his confidence. If you give time to your friends but also show you value and enjoy your son because you preserve time for him, he will get the true measure of the value you attach to him. Having and enjoying your friends therefore offers a double benefit, provided they don't crowd him out.

Parents

* 'I've had a lovely day with my friends, and now I'm having a lovely time with you. Aren't I lucky?'

* if you take your son with you when you meet friends, make sure he feels involved either in the group or with something you take for him to do

* be careful if you collect your younger children from school that they don't feel ignored as they emerge because you are deep in conversation with others. Greet them warmly each time

* enjoyment occurs when we engage with the present, the here and now

Teachers

* enjoy your students by talking to them as you see them around the building between lessons

* take time to enjoy yourself with colleagues in the staff room rather than working continuously

99 Endorse yourself

Children reap dividends when parents are comfortable with themselves. This entails accepting personal histories and the decisions that have been made, or not made, in earlier years. We should not continue to beat ourselves up for anything that happened or put the shutters down on the past and pretend that certain events did not happen. The more content we feel with ourselves, the less we will be tempted to relive or deny things through our children and the more we will be able to support and encourage them in healthy ways that reflect and give space to their true selves.

If we think we are not valuable or nothing we do is ever good enough, it is tempting to fill the emptiness that we feel inside with our son's successes or failures, and too easy to fashion an identity based on those, and to mould him to suit. If we don't feel good enough, we are likely to be more demanding of success and more grudging in giving praise, waiting until we feel it is really deserved. If he makes a mistake, we could feel it as a reflection on us, so we may either undermine the importance of the event or criticise him to protect our self-image.

Parents

* write down your strong points

* identify your regrets. But every cloud has a silver lining; nothing is ever a total disaster. For every decision or event you regret in the past, try to identify a positive personal trait or outcome that arose from it

* think of everything you have done to help others. Achievement is not just scored by publicly accepted measures

Teachers

* write down your professional strengths and enjoy and cherish these attributes

* list your weaker traits and consider how much they genuinely set you back

* consider how much you pressure your students to cover up your feared weaknesses

* try to accept that school should help students to thrive academically and socially and to mature in many ways. Recall instances when you have helped a student cope and develop, not just pass the exams

100 Encourage yourself

Good parenting is not about perfection because it is impossible to get it absolutely right all the time. In any case, people differ in their views about what is the right, or best, response for any situation, so it is not a practical goal. We make mistakes as parents – lots of them – just as growing boys do. We need encouraging pats on the back for doing our best: for trying new and more positive ways to say things to our sons; for trying to understand more about how they think and learn and about parent-child relationship dynamics – just as boys need encouragement. Our intentions and efforts are important; and these will often be enough to bring about noticeable changes in attitude and performance that need to be recognised in order to encourage further self-enhancing changes.

The future must look enticing. We are doing well enough and we can make changes to make the future look rosier. Our boys can and will do well and we should help them to imagine and expect a positive future by creating an atmosphere of hope, belief and appreciation for everyone in the family, in the here and now.

Parents

* setbacks are normal – part of the ebb and flow of life. The future will be bright, and we will feel more encouraged if we try some of the tips in this book

* don't beat yourself up: apply the recommended 4:1 praise to criticism / blame ratio to yourself. Every time you think you fall short, find four things to do or that you have already done that you can feel pleased about

* 'true power does not reveal itself' (Foucault, French philosopher). Providing a home in which each individual is empowered and able to explore their potential, quirks and interests without pressure and intrusive guidance is the healthy way forward

Teachers

* teaching is part of your life but not all of it. Think of all the other ways to accept and evaluate yourself – community or church activist, parent, partner, son or daughter – and be positive about your overall contribution

* be encouraged – the future is almost always rich and rosy if you open yourself to opportunities and think positive!

Postscript

In case you have reached the end of the book and feel a little swamped and confused by the 'oughts' and 'buts', having read it straight through, here are some suggestions and summaries.

Taking a broad view, far more children suffer today from not being praised enough than are being damaged by excessive or misplaced praise. Children have a profound need not only to be noticed by the close adults in their life but also to be affirmed, appreciated and enjoyed. Spending time with children can be difficult when everyone is so pressured, but all efforts to do so will be amply rewarded with warmth and love from a child who feels secure, loved and self-confident and wants, and knows how, to have fun as well as do well.

It is said that we remember a maximum of 10 per cent of what we hear or read at any one time. Having been faced with 100 tips and many more bullets, it might help to order your thoughts by writing down ten things that have remained clear and on which you could take action. Select some for a 'good things to do' list and some for a 'best avoided' group. Prioritise these, try them out over a few days and then dip into the book again to expand your repertoire from these experiences. Some will work for you, some may not. The important guidance is to use strategies that you feel comfortable with provided, of course, your son responds well to them and there are happy results all round.